TWAYNE'S WORLD AUTHORS SERIES

A Survey of the World's Literature

Sylvia E. Bowman, Indiana University

GENERAL EDITOR

FRANCE

Maxwell A. Smith, Guerry Professor of French, Emeritus
The University of Chattanooga
Visiting Professor in Modern Languages
The Florida State University

EDITOR

Alfred de Vigny

(TWAS 18)

Alfred de Vigny

By JAMES DOOLITTLE
University of Rochester

Twayne Publishers, Inc.   ::   New York

21134

THIS BOOK IS DEDICATED
TO
JOHN HAMBLET

Preface

The purpose of this book is to present to general readers, and especially to those who are not altogether confident of their French, an account of the work of Alfred de Vigny. Biographical information is included only to the extent that the present writer thought it pertinent to an understanding of that work. The same is true of information in the areas of history and of poetical tradition. A relatively lengthy summary of these latter was thought desirable, since up-to-date general works in English on these subjects in a French context are not easily available.

Some of Vigny's works are here examined in detail; others in summary; still others are barely mentioned. At the risk of seeming whimsical, the writer has on occasion paid scrupulous attention to some deservedly negligible items, while giving only passing notice to certain others customarily considered either as masterpieces or as mines richly salted with nuggets of great value for the specialist's understanding of his poet. This book's procedure arises from neither whimsy nor prejudice, but, as its text declares, from the opinion that Vigny is interesting not only because he wrote some unforgettable verse, but also because his writings, his career, provide an excellent display of a self-conscious artist in the process, first of becoming a master, and then of working as one. The documents herein examined have been chosen with the intention of illustrating this process.

The person of Vigny conforms in no way to either of the traditional caricatures of "the Romantic"; he was neither a dandy nor a beatnik. He was a gentleman in all of the senses of the word in his time, and in most of those given it in our own. The poet Vigny, in his growth, his becoming, and his mastery, was thoroughly Romantic; more important still, he was thoroughly and conscientiously a poet; and it is this fact which our book pretends to illustrate.

JAMES DOOLITTLE

University of Rochester

Contents

Chronology

1797 March 27	Vigny born at Loches (Indre-et-Loire).
1814 July 26	Sub-lieutenant in 1st Regiment of Gendarmes du Roi (Compagnies Rouges).
1815 March 20–June 28	The Hundred Days.
June 18	Waterloo.
1816 July 25	Death of Vigny's father.
1820 December	Article in *Le Conservateur littéraire* on an edition of Byron's works. Vigny's first publication.
1822 March	*Poèmes* published. Vigny's first book.
June	Victor Hugo, *Odes et poésies diverses*. Hugo's first collection.
1825 February 3	Marriage to Lydia Bunbury at Pau (Basses-Pyrénées).
1826 March	*Cinq-Mars.*
1826	*Poèmes antiques et modernes.*
1829 May	*Poèmes antiques et modernes* (augmented).
October 24	Premiere of *Le More de Venise* (*Othello*).
1830 February 25	Premiere of Hugo's *Hernani.*
July 27–29	Revolution, flight of Charles X; Louis-Philippe installed as "King of the French" (7 August).
1831 April–May	*L'Alméh*, in *Revue des deux mondes*.
June 25	Premiere of *La Maréchale d'Ancre*.
1832 June	*Stello.*
1835 February 12	Premiere of *Chatterton*.
October	*Servitude et grandeur militaires.*
1837	*Poèmes antiques et modernes* (definitive edition).

	December 21	Death of Vigny's mother.
1838	August	Final break with Marie Dorval.
	November	Death of Vigny's father-in-law. Residence in England, mostly in London, for some six months.
1843	January 15	*La Sauvage*, in *Revue des deux mondes* (*RDM*).
	February 1	*La Mort du loup*, in *RDM*.
	March 15	*La Flûte*, in *RDM*.
1844	June 1	*Le Mont des oliviers*, in *RDM*.
	July 15	*La Maison du Berger*, in *RDM*.
1845	May 8	Vigny elected to French Academy.
1846	January 29	Ceremony of reception into French Academy.
1848	February	February Revolution. Abdication of Louis-Philippe. Second Republic.
	December	Louis-Napoleon elected president.
1848–1853		Vigny resident at family estate, Le Maine-Giraud (Charente). Stood twice (1848 and 1849) for election to the Chamber of Deputies; defeated both times.
1851	December 2	Coup d'état. Louis-Napoleon dictator.
1852	November	Plebiscite. Louis-Napoleon becomes Napoleon III.
1854	February 1	*La Bouteille à la mer*, in *RDM*.
1862	December 22	Death of Mme de Vigny.
1863	September 16	Death of Vigny (cancer).
1864		*Les Destinées*, published by Ratisbonne.
1867		*Le Journal d'un poète*, published by Ratisbonne.
1912		*Daphné*, published by F. Gregh in *Revue de Paris*.

CHAPTER 1

Matrix

I *The Bourbon Restoration*

THE lifetime of Alfred de Vigny (1797–1863) spans almost exactly that period which historians of French literature customarily label Romantic. Between the publication of Chateaubriand's *Génie du christianisme* in 1802 and that of Baudelaire's revised *Les Fleurs du mal* in 1861, there was produced in France a body of writing unexampled there in volume and variety, if not, for the most part, in depth or originality. The crop thus harvested had been sown in the eighteenth century; it had been fertilized by the importation of forms and colors from the Middle Ages, of ideas and other materials from Britain and Germany, Italy, North Africa and the Near East (the "Orient," in contemporary terms), the South Seas, and America. It had been cultivated by the generation which, having come to adulthood in the eighteenth century, did its important work in the nineteenth— such, for example, as Chateaubriand, Benjamin Constant, Charles Nodier, Mme de Staël, Cuvier, Lamarck, Champollion, and Napoleon Bonaparte. It was brought to full fruition by the children of the new regime, those whose birth coincided, or nearly, with the birth of the nineteenth century: Lamartine (1790), Cousin (1792), Vigny (1797), Delacroix and Michelet (1798), Balzac (1799), Hugo and the elder Dumas (1802), Berlioz (1803), Sainte-Beuve and George Sand (1804), Musset (1810), and Gautier (1811). Indeed, among the figures of the first importance for French Romanticism, only four were born outside of this twenty-year period: Saint-Simon (1760), Lammenais and Stendhal (1782), and Baudelaire (1821).

Romantic thought, art, and literature are thus represented in the work of persons who, for the most part, were emerging from adolescence as the Restoration of the Bourbons was emerging from the First Empire. To these young people, the Revolution was a legend of injustice and violence, of horror and blood; the Empire was an intoxicating spectacle of glory and ambition which was nonetheless, as one began to think about it, the outgrowth of the Revolution. Yet the dream remained. The Empire had seemed to open the way of glory to meritorious service, to recognize and reward heroism without inquiring into the pedigree or the fortune of the hero. And it had certainly provided ample opportunity for some kinds of heroes. The Restoration of the Bourbons was welcomed as a return to legitimacy, to be sure, but not as a return to peace and quiet, still less as a revival of the old order in which eminence could be reached only through preferment. The constitution should mean that opportunity would remain democratized and that merit would duly be rewarded. There also appeared to be no lack of occasions for heroism, military and other.

But the young people had reckoned without their elders. The Bourbons clearly deplored the constitution as a necessary nuisance to be circumvented whenever possible. The old nobility vigorously sought the re-establishment of its prerogatives, alleging their violation, together with the inconveniences and hardships of emigration, as so many loyal services for which it now demanded recompense. The Napoleonic nobility, walking with soft circumspection, largely succeeded in maintaining itself. The bourgeoisie, industrialized and made prosperous by the Empire, mistrusted adventure and cared most of all for the stability implied in the return to legitimacy. Both because of the constitution, which, like its predecessor of the First Republic, was made very much in his favor, and because the regime needed his money, the bourgeois found his wishes respected. The claims of adventure and of merit were loudly outshouted by those of rank, money, and expedient security. All too rapidly under the Restoration, it became evident that this was a poor season for heroes.

Something of the fervor and the approaching disenchantment of the young Romantics is visible in the series of editions of Hugo's earliest collection of verse, his *Odes*, which appear in 1822, 1824, 1826, and 1828. The 1822 book displays a court poet, somewhat after the fashion, if not in the style, of a Malherbe,

dedicating his efforts to the glorification of the monarchy and
of its established religion. Here are eleven odes, written between
1818 and 1822, of which the first presents the function of the
"Poet in Revolutions": he will not remain aloof from the misfortunes of others; rather, "a voluntary exile upon earth, he consoles
sad humans in their chains; armed with his lyre, he thrusts himself among the frenzied peoples like Orpheus in the midst of
Hades." [1] The Poet marches ardently toward the future, "ani-
mated by a very God. . . . He prepares himself for sacrifice; he
knows that the happiness of vice is expiated by the innocent.
. . . The prison is his sanctuary, and the scaffold is his tripod!"
He seeks not repose, but honor, "heavenly martyrdom. . . . It is
to glory that I aspire. . . . For the eaglet, child of storms, it is
only through the clouds that he takes flight towards the sun!"

The working out of this noble aspiration provides us next with
lamentations for various defeated opponents of the Revolution,
an ode to the martyred Louis XVII, whom God addresses, by
way of conclusion, as follows: "Come, thy Lord himself had
his divine griefs, and my Son, like thee, a king crowned with
thorns, bore the reed sceptre!" There are odes on the death by
assassination of the Duc de Berry, nephew of Louis XVIII, and
two more on the birth and the christening of Berry's posthumous
son, the Duc de Bordeaux, who was to become Henri V of
France, despoiled of his birthright, in the legitimist view, by
the enthronement of Orleans in the person of Louis-Philippe.
And the book closes with two more poems: one, a "Vision" of
the eighteenth century brought before God and cast into eternity
after a vain attempt at a sort of *amende honorable;* the other,
entitled "Buonaparte" (*sic*), presents the career of the very
recently deceased emperor as that of a sort of unwitting scourge
of God which, having served the divine purpose, should now
be decently forgotten. The proper pudicity of young Orpheus
in this conclusion is perhaps overshadowed by some of the
finest writing in the book as certain of Attila's exploits are dwelt
upon almost lovingly.

Hugo's prefaces of 1822 (he wrote one in June and the other
in December) give us a satisfactory notion, if not an altogether
precise expression, of what he then thought poetry was, or should
be. In June he says that the publication of his book has two
intentions, "the literary one and the political one; but, in the

author's view, the latter is the consequence of the former, for poetry in the history of mankind can be seen and judged only from the heights of monarchical ideas and religious beliefs." [2]

Poetry's domain is boundless [he goes on]; beneath the real world, there exists a world of ideas [*un monde idéal*], which shows itself resplendent to the eye of those who have become accustomed by serious meditations to see in things more than things. The fair works of poetry of all kinds, in verse or in prose, which have honored our century, have revealed this truth, heretofore scarcely suspected, that poetry resides not in the form of the ideas, but in the ideas themselves.

In December he reprints the June preface, and adds notably that "every writer, in whatever field, should have as his principal objective to be useful"; thus Hugo "has tried to solemnize some of the principal memories of our period which may be lessons for future societies"; he has chosen to adapt the ode form, "substituting for the worn-out and false colors of pagan mythology the new and true colors of Christian theogony," thinking that he could thereby "put into the ode something of the interest of the drama, and make it speak, moreover, the austere, consoling and religious language needed by an old society which is still totteringly emerging from saturnalia of atheism and anarchy." [3]

The poet, in other words, sees through facts to the ideas that underlie them; these ideas are the substance of poetry, to be judged according to monarchical and Christian standards, and to be expressed in a language appropriate to monarchy and Christianity. These things are done in order that present society may be consoled and future societies instructed. In the preface to the next edition (1824) of the *Odes*, these notions are reiterated, and a new note, that of prophecy (which betrays, incidentally, an increasing frustration), is struck:

The literature of today, as it has been created by the Chateaubriands, the Staëls, the Lammenais', belongs in no way to the revolution. Just as the sophistical and lawless writings of the Voltaires, the Diderots and the Helvétius' were the advance expression of the social innovations which flowered in the decrepitude of the last century, so today's literature . . . is the foreshadowing expression of the religious and monarchical society which will *undoubtedly* emerge from so many old and recent ruins. It must be said over and over again: what is torturing our minds is not a need for novelty, but a need for truth, and the need is immense. [4]

Apparently it is the poet's task to supply the need. He must apply himself "above all to repairing the harm wrought by the sophists. . . . He must go on before the peoples like a light and show them the way. . . . His songs will celebrate unceasingly the glories and the misfortunes of his country, the austerities and the delights of his religion." [5]

"Undoubtedly" suggests doubt; a cry for truth shows an awareness of falsehood. The situation is not bright. Present glories seem rather scarce; the poet must do the best he can with a paucity of available materials. The Spanish war of 1823 is made to serve (Book II, Ode VII, dated November, 1823); this was the not very arduous struggle whereby Ferdinand VII was resettled on his throne as an absolute ruler and the 1812 constitution of the Spanish Cortes was annulled (the constitution's defect, says Hugo in a footnote to his poem, was that it "was modeled upon our constitution of 1792"). For genuine glory, the urge to look to Napoleon in spite of everything is becoming more and more obviously irresistible. "La Guerre d'Espagne" is followed immediately in Book II by the ode to the Arc de Triomphe de l'Étoile, also dated November, 1823, from which we learn that, reprehensible as he may have been, Napoleon was still glorious and French. Book III dutifully sings the nation's disaster in "Les Funérailles de Louis XVIII," which is of course followed by the even greater hope of glory symbolized in "Le Sacre [coronation]de Charles X." But the outstanding piece in this book (and one of Hugo's great poems) is the hymn to "La Colonne de la Place Vendôme" (February, 1827). Let those who threaten France with dishonor remember her "two giants," Charlemagne and Napoleon, and beware of offending her. But the defiance is cast in the name of past glory; the present is "this age of waiting," in which we Frenchmen are "eaglets banished from the sky, condemned to peace; let us at least, as wary sentinels watching over paternal glories, be sure to guard the arms of our fathers from any insult." The sulky defiance of the present at the close of this poem emphasizes the splendor of the emperor, misguided though he was, which is the substance of this hymn of praise. The court poet has not been seen since Charles X's coronation, nor will he appear again.

As Hugo's admiration passes from the Bourbons to the memory of Napoleon, so does his awareness of the world and its problems become deeper and more complex. The simple rights

and wrongs of morals and politics as seen by the devoted royalist have given place to complexities and nuances. The scourge,
the false god Buonaparte has become an "unapproachable sphinx
. . . at once monster and god ("Fin," Book III, Ode VIII, May,
1828). The poet's mission remains; it is now perhaps even more
urgent because of the inefficiency of monarchy and church. For
this reason also the poet must seek elsewhere the means to its
fulfillment.

Hugo's progress in the third decade of the century is by no
means identical with Vigny's; at the same time, it represents,
in its shift from an easy royalism through increasing disillusionment to a thoughtful searching for other values and other means
of expression, and also in its constant faith in the high calling of
the poet, the crisis of loyalties and convictions undergone by
Vigny and most of his generation in the same decade. Less
reserved than Vigny, perhaps more *naïf*, and certainly more
productive in this period, Hugo furnishes a documentation of the
crisis which seems to me somehow the more interesting because
it is outspoken and published in verse.

II *The Roots of the Romantic Prophecy*

The fairest fruits of Romantic literature, at least in retrospect,
are lyrical in substance and also in form. There is general agree-
ment that the greatest lyrists of the first half of the century are
four: Lamartine, Hugo, Vigny, and Musset. And while all four
did outstanding work in various genres of prose and verse, it is
their lyrical writings which come first to mind when their names
are mentioned. In lyric verse they can (and do) boast of being
pioneers as well as the leaders of their generation; under their
hands the old forms—song, ode, ballad, sonnet, elegy (elegy
above all)—were adjusted and reshaped into instruments amen-
able to the performance of a music composed upon a new mode.

Romanticism is a word notoriously incapable of precise definition. Yet, in deference to a historical tradition which compels
us to call Vigny a Romantic writer, we must try to give some
account of it. The effort seems especially called for in a study
intended primarily for English-speaking readers, since English
Romanticism and French Romanticism, despite many common
characteristics and terms, are in many ways dissimilar.[6] Without

comparing the two traditions, let me describe the general growth of the French one as briefly as a concern for present adequacy allows.

Romanticism is a child of the French eighteenth century, that period so misleadingly called the Age of Reason. Especially does it grow from *la philosophie,* a phenomenon which, properly speaking, is not philosophy, but an unsystematic exploration of the nature of man and of his relationships to other men and to the physical universe. This effort begins in iconoclasm and leads, in theory at least, to freedom. The freedom provided for in the Declaration of the Rights of Man, for one thing. Freedom, speaking more generally, from metaphysics, from the authority of divine right and all of the beliefs, traditions, and sanctions implied in that doctrine. Freedom to reject, on the basis of the new science epitomized in the work of Bacon, Newton, and Locke, the anthropocentric hypothesis, and to deny the heavy moral responsibilities implied in the notion of man's divinely given rulership of nature. Freedom to examine, to apply the method of Descartes beyond the limits discreetly imposed by Descartes, to accumulate and combine data from whatever sources, and from this procedure to arrive at whatever conclusions, untrammeled by miracles or other supernatural considerations. Freedom, in a word, for every man to observe, think, believe, speak, and act as he sees fit, subject only to the physical limitations imposed by his organism and its surroundings, and the moral ones imposed by his conscience.

Conscience is founded upon knowledge, and for *la philosophie,* which accepts the gospel according to John Locke, the sole beginning of knowledge is sensation. The organism senses; sensations are stored in the memory; it is the function of reason and imagination alike to combine present and remembered sensations into patterns. Reason also presides over, and then accedes to, experimental testing of these patterns; these, if proved valid in fact, become items of knowledge.

Of the two pattern-forming faculties, reason is confined by the necessity for experimental proof; the latter in turn is limited by the imperfection of available instruments. Imagination is subject to no such restriction. Its patterns may far exceed the verifying capacity of existing instruments. These patterns may be no more than illusions, hallucinations, madness; the fascinating possibility nonetheless remains that they may one day, given improved instruments, be verified. *La philosophie* observes that history records many such occurrences, wherefore many more may be expected. Imagination thus becomes the faculty of prophecy.

The age of *la philosophie* is an age of transition, a period of uncertainty, of groping. The breaking up of the old sanctions is clearly and amply stated. One often knows very precisely what one does not believe or believe in. But the formulation of a new faith is more difficult. *La philosophie* finds itself in this situation, and for this reason especially, perhaps, it comes to prize the prophet above all other kinds of men. Rather than call him "prophet," it chooses to give him a new name, fittingly enough elevating for this purpose a word which had previously meant merely "aptitude." Encouraged no doubt by English usage already current early in the century, *la philosophie* calls its prophet *l'homme de génie,* "the man of genius."

La philosophie was firmly committed to the doctrine of progress. It believed that the passage of time inevitably brings with it increase of knowledge; the day must therefore come when man will have acquired all knowledge and will thus incarnate the perfection of God. To add to the sum of knowledge is a man's noblest accomplishment; the most exalted of men is thus he who does this most and best, and this is the man of genius.

This prophet is a person extraordinarily well endowed in body and mind, possessed of keen sensitivity, capacious memory, acute reason, and rich and active imagination. Among these faculties, imagination must dominate. The function of the man of genius is to penetrate, by means of the patterns which his imagination and reason create, beyond the realm of present knowledge to a vision of things as yet unknown, and so to give expression to his insights as to make them comprehensible and subject sooner or later to verification by his less well-endowed fellow men. His vision is of his making; his proper activity may thus be called creative; and *la philosophie* comes increasingly to give to the man of genius the name of creator: it calls him "poet," irrespective of field or medium. For example, Plato, Homer, Michelangelo, Newton, Richardson—all are poets.

Prophet, man of genius, poet: all of these terms designate the man of creative insights dedicated to the service of mankind.

He is the most useful, the most beneficial, of men. He, more than anyone else, contributes to the sum of knowledge and hence to the formation of conscience. And because his insights, transgressing the bounds of present knowledge, may cause him as well to violate existing conventions of behavior and doctrine, he is likely to be of all men the least understood and the least appreciated by most other men. To them he must often seem a rebel, an enemy, or, at best, a milksop visionary or a madman. Aware of his peculiar destiny, he may glory in it, and rightly; it is more likely that, aware or unaware of it, he will be miserable.

La philosophie produced this conception of the poet out of a notion of human nature which tended to abrogate the traditional Christian dualism of spirit and flesh. No longer were these elements seen as being heterogeneous, still less as being at war with each other, the flesh contradicting, vitiating, corrupting, and degrading the spirit. Now they had become but two aspects of a single essence. Their indispensability one to the other was no longer a cause for lamentation, a punishment for miraculous and unjust original depravity, a symbol of damnation. Rather, the essential oneness of a human being was seen as the fundamental determinant of ultimate triumph. The traditionally denigrated flesh, its vulnerability, its feelings, appetites, emotions, passions, illusions, now functioned to nourish and energize the "spiritual" activity by which man must inevitably fulfill his destiny and arrive at the perfection of godhead, thus achieving the happiness to whose pursuit *la philosophie* asserted, for the first time in the Christian era, his "inalienable right."

La philosophie as a palpable ideological climate belongs to the second half of the eighteenth century. For convenience we may date its efflorescence between 1751 (the publication of the first volume of the *Encyclopédie* which is its epitome) and 1794, when the Terror ended with the execution of Robespierre (July 27 or 9 Thermidor *An* II). Its greatest theorists and exponents were dead well before 1789: Montesquieu (1755), Voltaire and Rousseau (1778), Diderot (1784). They were survived by a host of lesser lights and imitators, outstanding among them Beaumarchais, who created Figaro, Bernardin de Saint-Pierre, Condorcet, Mirabeau, and Robespierre. Only two stars shine brightly in the literary sky of the century's last decade: the Marquis de Sade and André Chénier.

Sade's systematic nihilism is a beautifully written and unanswerable testimonial to the ethical bankruptcy of eighteenth-century society;[7] it provides a fitting conclusion to an era of philosophical exploration carried out upon deterministic principles amid social and political realities characterized by appalling confusion, cynicism, and inefficacy. *La philosophie* was systematic only in deploring all systems. Sade took it at its word and provided the final artistic representation of the consequences. His triumph was necessarily a sterile one; it had few imitators and no progeny. To some reflective spirits it may conveniently symbolize the Terror (*Justine, ou les malheurs de la vertu* is of 1791).

As a poet, meanwhile, André Chénier was aware that he lived in a time of transition in the progress of institutions and of poetry, and his work is a willing and successful endeavor to formulate and illustrate the principles of the moment. "Sur des pensers nouveaux faisons des vers antiques": deeply and expertly learned, unlike most of his contemporaries, in the literature and scholarship of all periods of ancient Greece, Greek himself by his mother, and an admirer of the formal achievements of his great predecessors of the age of Louis XIV, he was also a dedicated partisan of the ideas and interests of *la philosophie*, particularly as these are elaborated by Rousseau. His verse, like Rousseau's rhetoric, is meant to be a tried and proved "ancient" medium for expressing the new knowledge of man and of his expanded world and aspirations, for recording and criticizing the search for a new morality. As, for Rousseau, man's ultimate test for truth resides in his sentiment, so, for Chénier, the essence of poetry, that which distinguishes it from versification, is the presence of sentiment. "L'art ne fait que des vers, le coeur seul est poète" ("Technique merely makes verses; the heart alone is the poet")—so he enunciates his doctrine, which is indeed that of *la philosophie* in general. Chénier, who in 1794 was imprisoned and guillotined (two days before Robespierre) for pamphleteering, had thus a most poignant experience of some real applications of political principles, many of which, like those of both Chénier and his executioners, claimed the paternity of Rousseau. These circumstances, together with his authorship of the best and most passionate lyric verse of the eighteenth century, made of him an appropriate object for the admiration of the royalist-minded young poets of 1820. At the latter date, in fact, even his Greek blood was symbolic. Excellent craftsman in verse, erudite in the foundations of his art, partisan of the new knowledge and progressive ideas, pathetic victim of these ideas mistakenly and excessively applied, above all an articulate man of feeling, capable of both angelic tenderness and the most corrosive hatred, Chénier could be idolized by royalist, moderate, and liberal alike without compromising the political or poetical professions of any.

III *Politics and Romanticism*

Nineteenth-century French politics is inseparable from the birth of Romanticism. Of the works of Rousseau, its patron saint, its partisans knew the *Contrat social* and the *Émile* as well as they did the *Nouvelle Héloïse,* the *Rêveries d'un promeneur solitaire,* the *Confessions.* Chateaubriand, their nearer patron, nobleman, former *émigré,* ambassador of Louis XVIII at the Court of Saint James, future would-be vassal of Henri V, embodied conservatism. One of their principal textbooks, Mme de Staël's *De l'Allemagne* (1810), had been produced out of political opposition and exile. Born of the generation of the Revolution, adolescent in the Empire, come to manhood at the Restoration, cognizant as never before of its national identity and of the existence and the nature of its foreign neighbors, faced with unprecedented economic phenomena, newly sensitive to religious doubts and controversies, recently enfranchised, the best educated public yet to appear in France (and above all its literati) could not help being extraordinarily alive to the fascinating excitements and frustrations of politics. Then, as now, the French periodical press was political first, and whatever else it chose to be afterwards. The thirty years between 1790 and 1820 had witnessed a concentration of upheavals, a transformation from an old to a new world, not altogether dissimilar in profundity, violence, and scope to those undergone by our country in the past thirty years or so. Then, as now, there resulted vast uncertainty, with more desire than hope for secure and honorable refuge. Then, as now, both Right and Left formulated easy panaceas which were tried with enthusiasm and rapidly, by many, found wanting; and the search for new idols or articles of faith was resumed. And then, as now, for some, a new faith would eventually be found—in art. The progress of Romanticism ultimately accomplished (but only in the sixth decade of the century) a virtual divorcement of art from politics.

Romanticism both embodies many of the principles of *la philosophie* and reacts against many of its practices. In its turn, *la philosophie* had reacted against the authoritarianism of the age of Louis XIV, but its revolt was one less of form than of content or substance. Of all European nations, France is undoubtedly the most stubbornly enduring in its adherence to cultural formalism, and nowhere is this more apparent than in its literature. In no other country is there quite the equivalent to the real continuity of literary tradition symbolized by the French Academy and coincident with the history of that body. The Academy was founded in 1635 by Richelieu to serve primarily a political purpose: the centralization of all power and authority in the throne. Within two years it had consolidated itself by taking sides and winning in a literary quarrel, and the side it took was that of rule against public acceptance and individual taste. Most of the foremost literary men in France have begun their careers and achieved their fame as opponents of the Academy; a very large number of them have died members of it.

Literary quarrels tend to interest a wider and proportionally more numerous audience in France than in most other countries. Literary doctrines, codifications of past practices, recipes for future ones are debated both in academic gatherings and in the press, and also in that other sociocultural institution brought in France to its highest degree of perfection—the *salon*. The authority of taste which results is by no means abstract; it can and frequently does make or break the success of the aspiring artist or intellectual. He may accept or resist it, but he ignores it on peril of nonentity.

The preoccupations of the taste-forming institutions are inevitably as much political as they are esthetic; at certain historical moments they are much more so. The years of the Restoration mark one of these moments. The arts and literature, regardless of opinion or party, were then seen as the servants of society. Literary doctrines had to subserve political and social ends. The striking success of that new departure in poetry, Lamartine's *Méditations poétiques* (five editions in 1820 alone), owes more than a little to its royalist and Catholic convictions. This book was hailed in its own time as a monument, and we still consider it one; but we prize it far more for its marvelously harmonious expressions of sentiment than for the ideological content which made its reputation with many of its contemporaries. These last were wont to set Lamartine's poems up against the "atheism" of Byron, for example, in order to "prove," in the words of one conservative reviewer, "the degree to which sound doctrines in religion, politics, and literature are bound up together." [8] Taking their lead from Chateaubriand, the great majority of the promising young writers professed conservatism, an attitude intensified by the general reaction to the assassination of the Duc de Berry (1820); early in 1821 was formed the Société des Bonnes-Lettres, whose membership included, in addition to Chateaubriand and many other literate members of the royalist aristocracy, Lamartine, Victor Hugo and his two brothers, Nodier, Emile Deschamps, Soumet, Vigny—nearly all the writers whose names would be in the forefront of the Romantic triumph of 1830.

As the decade of the 1820's wore on, there emerged an approximate identification of literary with political and religious doctrines. Classicism, the imitation of the Ancients under the patronage of Reason, somehow represented the thirty years of Revolution and Empire which terminated the Age of Reason; and it became the shibboleth of liberalism. Romanticism simultaneously was coming into common usage as a label for the conservative principles intended to ensure in all endeavors the continuity of royalist France. These identifications, however, prove to be misleading, especially the latter one. No sooner were they made than political partisanship began to yield, as we have seen it do in Hugo, to increasing maturity and political disenchantment. The rising generation came rapidly to seek its salvation in independence and originality.

The triumph of French Romanticism is customarily dated in 1830, to coincide with the successful first performance of Hugo's *Hernani* at the Comédie Française (February 25). This event had been in preparation, so to speak, for some three years. The younger writers and artists of the Société des Bonnes-Lettres had become, in 1824, the core of the more famous grouping in the *salon* of Charles Nodier at the Arsenal library. Though this assemblage was royalist, with little or no liberal representation, in doctrine it could not at first be called a school. With the passage of time and the succession of events, however, the young people tended more and more to neglect the urbane and tolerant eclecticism of Nodier's leadership for the increasingly doctrinary and militant domination of one of themselves. This was Victor Hugo, whose growing independence of literary and political orthodoxy was matched by the blooming of a conscious ambition to be the chief of a new school. This ambition began to be realized in his formation in 1827 of the famous *Cénacle* of Romanticism. Around him in his own house he gathered what since has become recognized as the complete roster of Romantic genius (except Stendhal): the poets Lamartine, Vigny, Sainte-Beuve (who would presently turn to criticism), Émile Deschamps; the artists Delacroix, Deveria, David d'Angers; the more recent recruits to the new ideas: Gérard de Nerval, the elder Dumas, Mérimée, Balzac, Musset. It was in this *Cénacle* that Romanticism was constituted as a school. Its doctrines were being elaborated and were appearing in such pieces as Hugo's prefaces to his play *Cromwell* (1827) and his *Odes et ballades* (1828), Sainte-Beuve's *Tableau historique et critique* of the French poetry and drama of the sixteenth century (1828), Vigny's *Lettre à Lord . . .* on the occasion of the premiere of his translation of *Othello* (1829). And the theoretical presentations were accompanied or soon followed by works intended to exemplify them: Hugo's *Orientales,* Dumas' drama *Henri III et sa cour,* Vigny's *Othello,* and Hugo's *Marion de Lorme* and *Hernani.*

Having, as it happened, forced some tolerance of the new practices upon the press and even upon the Academy, the young men directed their ultimate assault upon the most stubborn stronghold of orthodoxy, the Comédie Française. Here, as elsewhere, but more obviously, the claims of long-standing convention were abetted by those of ignorance and vested interest (to say nothing of control—hence censorship—by the royal authority). The company accepted a play by majority vote of its members, subject to ministerial or royal approval. By its very venerability, this company, the House of Molière, was convinced that its accustomed theatrical ways were right; new ways were met with extreme skepticism. This theater was, moreover, a respected national institution; as such it must be very sensitive to criticism made in the name of the nation and its mores. Add to all that the very palpable personal interests existing within a group of established and subsidized virtuosos, and it becomes plain that powerful leverage was necessary in order to bring about alterations of its tradition.

By good fortune for the Romantic cause, the royal commissioner for the Comédie Française was the baron Taylor (appointed July 9, 1825). As he began his task, the national theater was in a situation verging upon disaster, cultural and financial. Taylor was a man of sophistication and also of discretion. By no means unsympathetic to the innovators (he participated in the gatherings at the Arsenal as well as in Hugo's *Cénacle*), he tempered his enthusiasm with hard, practical sense and a certain diplomatic skill. By a combination of soft talk and authority, he was able to procure the company's acceptance of plays written more or less in the new idiom. He also used the prestige of his charge to calm the misgivings of the censors. As early as November, 1825, aided no doubt by the popularity of the current revolt in Greece, he successfully mounted the somewhat unorthodox *Léonidas* of Pichat, an event which earned him the compliments even of Talma, the leading actor of the national troupe. Talma and his colleagues were nevertheless far from being converted; in the name of good theatrical practice, they continued to obstruct the performance of works of the new order.

The theater was not only a bastion of the old esthetic regime; it was also the emporium for the most popular art forms of its time. Its audience was more heterogenous, more passionate, and more vocal than that of any other medium. Hugo and his group thought, as indeed did everyone else, that the solid establishment of their school could be completed only by conquering the theater. The years 1827 to 1830 were largely given over by them to a definite campaign to this end.

The patron saints of the classical theater in France are Corneille, Racine, and Voltaire in tragedy, Molière in comedy. Their plays, or at any rate those which are habitually cited for the needs of the classical cause, are in verse, in five acts, in the heroic meter which consists of rhyming couplets of the twelve-syllable Alexandrine line. The regular Alexandrine contains a caesura after the sixth syllable and a pause (comma or full stop) at the end of the line. Run-on lines are rare and to be used only with the greatest discretion, as are displacements of the caesura. The style of these plays is "elevated" for high comedy, "sublime" for tragedy; their vocabulary must avoid the "baseness," the "vulgarity," of common speech (as late as 1837, Hugo could still shock conservative critics by naming a poem *La Vache* [cow] instead of using the elevated—and inaccurate— *Génisse* [heifer]). The subject matter of tragedy is the struggle of the extraordinary man—prince, hero, demi-god chosen from ancient history or legend—against destiny; that of comedy is the "vices" of ordinary (i.e., bourgeois) society. There must be no mingling of styles or genres within a single play; the high seriousness of tragedy must not be corrupted by any hint of lightness, of "comic relief." Costumes and scene-settings are conventional, paying little or no respect to historical accuracy. Local color is ignored; stage directions are virtually nonexistent. Above all, these plays, comedy and tragedy alike, must observe the famous unities of place, time, and action: one setting, one day, one plot.

Voltaire, it is true, had attempted to loosen somewhat the rigidity of these regulations, notably by demanding the use of comparatively modern subjects (French, American, Christian) and a care for historical verisimilitude; and he sought, and to some extent obtained, the substitution of a relatively naturalistic manner of stage action and declamation for the prevalent conventional symmetry. He had also, and with enthusiasm, discovered Shakespeare and made his name known in France. But, as the eighteenth century's leading apostle of classical taste, he saw Shakespeare's works as a welter of barbarism punctuated by moments of genius. This was the universal French judgment of Shakespeare in the eighteenth century, and it persisted into the nineteenth.

By the same token, Shakespeare's theater became the principal rallying point for the new school's campaign. No French playwright had approached the freedom and the technical and poetic mastery of Shakespeare. His acceptance by the French theatrical public would be a sure presage of the establishment of Romanticism. He had been frequently "translated" since the middle of the eighteenth century; these versions were invariably purged of his "barbarisms" and made to conform to the prescriptions of French taste. It was, moreover, obviously impossible to render in French the incomparable poetry of the original. A presentation in English was thus desirable, and in 1822 a somewhat inept English company made the attempt in Paris with *Othello*.[9] The attempt failed, partly because the memory of the humiliation at Waterloo was still painful. Shakespeare was denigrated by some as "an aide-de-camp of Wellington." At this date, in any case, the public was clearly unready, the press was hostile, and the literary leaders belonged to the Société des Bonnes-Lettres, which was dedicated to the preservation of good French taste.

Five years later another English troupe, headed by the able and diplomatic Macready, came to Paris to present Shakespeare and other English playwrights in the original. This time the effort was extremely successful. Intending at first to remain in France until December (1827), the troupe prolonged its stand into the middle of 1828, thus affording French audiences a full year of English drama. *Othello, Hamlet, Romeo and Juliet, Richard III* were very well received; *Macbeth, King Lear, The Merchant of Venice,* if less popular, still were not failures.

The French sojourn of Macready and his troupe is one of the cardinally important events in the history of French literature. It confirms the end of two and a half centuries of cultural chauvinism. More immediately, it made unmistakably evident the fact that the road to the Romantic conquest was now open.

The rest of the way was marked by a series of engagements, most of them Romantic victories, in close succession. In 1826 and 1827, Hugo wrote his monumental, intentionally unplayable drama *Cromwell,* together with its celebrated preface, which is the school's first great manifesto. Struck off now (in theory) are the classical fetters, the unities first and foremost; gone are the generic distinctions in form, style, and subject matter; the *bienséances,* the rather finicky proprieties of action and language, no longer exert authority. Tragedy, comedy, bourgeois drama, and even melodrama may now be brought together in a single production. All classes of men, all historical events, and all religions may fittingly be represented. Verisimilitude in characters, manners, dress, customs, settings, is demanded. Drama is proclaimed the art form most appropriate to modern times, as the lyric was to primitive ages, and the epic to that of heroism. The dramatic hero is no longer a typical or symbolic character only, but also an individual human being subject to the deformities and the vicissitudes imposed by reality. The play, for all its picturesqueness, must nevertheless transcend mere chronicle to incarnate the meditations of a thinker; it must be not a transposition, a photographic copy, but rather the poetization of a reality—its elevation, by means of art, to beauty, and hence to immortality.

The practice followed more or less closely, in time and in fact, upon the theory. In 1828, Hugo offered his *Amy Robsart,* dramatized out of *Kenilworth;* the play failed. In February, 1829, Dumas' *Henri III et sa cour,* in prose, succeeded at the Comédie Française and was presently followed by Vigny's verse translation of *Othello.* Hugo, who preferred verse to prose for the drama, and who thought that a French work would be a more telling weapon in the battle than a translation, in the same year completed his *Marion de Lorme,* only to have it forbidden by the censor. He then hastened to supply the deficiency with *Hernani,* whose epoch-making and very noisy premiere took place on February 25, 1830.

Thus victoriously established, the Romantic alliance lost no time in disintegrating. It had been rather factitious anyhow, a union born of the temporary suppression of disagreements, animosities, and conflicting ambitions, in the service of the cause. The battle won, the combatants took up or resumed divergent paths.

The Romantic drama would continue to flourish, notably in Hugo's hands, for another decade; the same decade would see the emergence of the pure lyricism of Musset in poetry and in armchair theater. In 1835, Théophile Gautier published, in *Mademoiselle de Maupin* and its preface, the manifesto of what would become Parnassianism, dedicated to the doctrine of art for art's sake. Already, in 1829, Balzac had published a novel, *Les Chouans,* which was somehow something more than the modish fusion of Scott and Fenimore Cooper that it appeared to be; he would ultimately include it, along with *Eugénie Grandet* (1833) and *Le Père Goriot* (1834) in the vast panorama of the *Comédie humaine.* In 1830, Stendhal, never a member of Hugo's coterie, brought out *Le Rouge et le noir.* With these works the realistic novel, the genre which would dominate nineteenth-century literature as tragedy had dominated that of the age of Louis XIV, was fairly launched.

The July Revolution was shortly preceded by the publication of the social doctrine of Saint-Simon (1829); it was shortly followed by Lammenais' sensational abjuration of the Church in the *Paroles d'un croyant* (1834); both made many disciples. The Romantic triumph of 1830 marked not only the demise of classicism but also the beginning of an intensive fermentation in all fields, one so active and so diverse as to defy precise classification or definition. The misguided reign of Charles X (1824–30), his overthrow by the July Revolution, the substitution of Orleans for Bourbon in the accession of Louis-Philippe posed cruel problems for the professed vassals of the restored regime. Their inclination now was toward independence. More than ever, they proclaimed the nation's need for truly poetic leadership; less and less did they seek in Bourbon tradition, less still among extant Bourbons, the bases or the models of that leadership. Restoration and Revolution alike became suspect, if not reprehensible, to them. A man after all is an individual; one should therefore reject all dogmas and place his reliance rather upon originality, upon his own beliefs, his personal interpretations of things religious, political, social, and esthetic, and of the relationships to be found among them.

Of all this, Alfred de Vigny was an interested witness and, often, a participant. By the nature of his personality as well as that of his thought and his work, he seems, even while participating, to stand apart. Like that of a Hugo, a Stendhal, a Balzac, a Musset, his figure is a dominant one in French Romanticism. Far more than the others, however, Vigny seems to be a man who is in his time, but not of it. As man and artist, he is at once an anachronism and a foreshadowing of the future.

CHAPTER 2

The Man and the Writer

I *Summary*

FOR the literate general public, Vigny came to prominence in his own time, and survives into ours, because of some of his verse. For his contemporaries, his name brought first to mind the author of *Eloa* and of *Moïse;* for us, who seldom read *Eloa,* he is the poet of *Moïse* and of *Les Destinées.* He also wrote plays, novels, and criticism, and he made excellent translations; yet it seems neither accurate nor fitting to consider him as being other than a poet. Victor Hugo, to be sure, is dramatist and novelist as well as poet; Lamartine, statesman and teacher; Sainte-Beuve, critic and essayist; Gérard de Nerval, journalist and translator. No writer has dedicated himself and his work more thoroughly or more exclusively to poetry than did Vigny. It is difficult to find in the canon of his writings, even in his diary and his correspondence, many items which do not directly concern themselves with poetry.

His written output is small, particularly in comparison to that of most of his contemporaries. In lyric and narrative poetry, it comprises the miniature epic *Eloa* (778 lines; 1824); two small collections: *Poèmes antiques et modernes,* whose fullest edition (1837) contains twenty poems, of which the longest has 332 lines; and the posthumous *Les Destinées* (1864), eleven poems, the longest containing 336 lines. Beyond these, the *Pléiade* edition[1] publishes some fifty occasional pieces and fragments, some of them very short, together with the almost obligatory epic on the Greek insurrection, *Héléna* (1822), which is the longest (924 lines) and one of the least satisfying of all of Vigny's poems.

Verse drama is represented by translations of *Othello* (*Le More de Venise,* 1829) and *The Merchant of Venice* (*Shylock,* unproduced and unpublished in Vigny's lifetime). Vigny also translated the last two acts of *Romeo and Juliet,* the first three having been rendered by Émile Deschamps; Vigny's part of this work was not produced. In addition, he planned, partly wrote, and then destroyed (1832) a tragedy on Roland, another on Antony and Cleopatra, and a third on Julian the Apostate.

His production in prose is likewise slender. For the stage, two dramas, *La Maréchale d'Ancre* (1831) and *Chatterton* (1835), and one *proverbe* (the genre soon to flower under the hand of Musset), *Quitte pour la peur* (1833). A historical novel, *Cinq-Mars* (1826), is done somewhat after the manner of Scott. Two other "novels," *Stello* (1832) and *Daphné* (unpublished until 1912), are not so much novels as they are philosophical ruminations fictionally illustrated. *L'Alméh* (1831) comprises the first four chapters of a projected novel on the French invasion of Egypt. Grouped under the title *Servitude et grandeur militaires* (1833–35) are three superb short stories which constitute Vigny's masterpiece in fiction and one of the great works of the century.

The list of prose writings, correspondence apart, is completed by a number of more or less critical pieces: a review of an edition of Byron's works, which is Vigny's earliest publication (1820); the "Réflexions sur la vérité dans l'art," which is the preface to *Cinq-Mars;* the "Lettre à Lord . . .," prefacing the translation of *Othello;* the "Dernière nuit de travail," introducing *Chatterton;* a memorial to the Chamber of Deputies, which in 1841 was debating a copyright law; the formal Discourse read by Vigny at his reception into the French Academy (1846); finally, the most voluminous and varied of all his prose, his journal, which runs from 1823 to 1863.[2] What has been said of this bibliography in general applies very particularly to the journal: virtually every line is preoccupied with the one subject, poetry. Few titles have been more happily chosen than that attached to its publication. Louis Ratisbonne, appointed by Vigny to execute his literary testament, called it the *Journal d'un Poète.*

II *Inheritance*

From first to last, the writings of Vigny are made in the service of a cause; more often than not, the cause is an idea. The use, for its own sake, of sentiment, of the picturesque, the exotic, the decorative, or the curious, is minimal in his work. He writes few equivalents to the *Ballades* or the *Orientales* of Hugo; his work provides no counterpart to the architectural tour of Paris in *Notre-Dame de Paris;* or to the Niagara Falls or the lower Mississippi landscapes of Chateaubriand. One looks in vain for any such display of purely technical gymnastics as Hugo's *Les Djinns.* Apart from a few occasional pieces, there is nothing of the personal expression of sentiment and gentle passion which is the essence of Lamartine's *Méditations.* Likewise missing are the ebullient or the tender songs of Musset and the apparently reckless, headlong, and exclusive passion which pervades Musset's lyricism. The soaring, flaming egotism of Hernani or Ruy Blas is not to be found in Vigny, any more than is the hermetism of a Gérard de Nerval or the lapidary precision of a Gautier. If Vigny is guilty of what looks to us like ill-judged topicality in a verse diatribe against rail transportation (*Maison du Berger,* 1844), his introduction of the mechanical monster is at least functional in the poem, and his treatment of it is restraint itself by comparison, for example, to Lamartine's detailed, ridiculous, and quite gratuitous aircraft (*La Chute d'un ange,* 1838). His remarkably faithful translations from Shakespeare are made in the service of Romantic freedom in the theater. His *Héléna,* unoriginal and inept as it is, propagates the cause of struggling Greece. Like the rest of his own work (as distinguished from the translations), *Héléna* is preoccupied with the nature and the functions of the leader of humanity, and this figure for Vigny is ideally the poet.

He inherits the notion of the poet as leader, prophet, and philosopher from Byron, Chateaubriand, and Goethe, as well as from *la philosophie.* For the detailed elaboration of the poet, his personality, his morality, his responsibility, his solitude, Vigny looks to himself. The misfit that he was coincides very well with the theoretical (and often historical) position of the creative genius. Unrecognized, uncomprehended, sometimes reviled and even persecuted, this superior being belongs in, but not to, his time, working in spite of everything for the benefit of mankind. In several senses, Vigny did not seem, at least to himself, to be of his time, and his persistent self-scrutiny led him perhaps to exaggerate his misplacement.

At his birth, his mother was forty years old, and his father sixty. He was reared as an only child by an invalid father and a very positive mother. Three brothers before him had died in infancy; Vigny never forgot that he was the last of his name and that that name was a noble one. The nobility of his family, on both sides, is undoubted, but its exact provenience is rather vague—a quality intensified by false pretensions made, knowingly or otherwise, to family alliances and titles. Vigny styled himself *comte* from his father's death until his own, but the claim was founded only upon demonstrably mistaken allegations of his father.

What is important for us is his pervasive awareness of the fact of his nobility. This was exacerbated by his growing up, from the age of eighteen months, in the Paris of the Directorate, the Consulate, and the Empire—a place and time full of uncertainties and frustrations, especially for a conscientious and practicing adherent of the Old Regime; nor was it made less acute by an annoying condition of poverty which needs must be borne with appropriate gentility. The invalidism of Vigny's father came from his military service in the Seven Years' War; like many Frenchmen of his generation (he was born in 1737), he had fought against and admired Frederick of Prussia, had been wounded and thereby reduced to a state of helplessness in which he could look only to the past for joy in life. This he did, aided by a talent for narration which utterly charmed his son. And the tales that he told seem invariably to have illustrated the feudal virtue of heroic, unquestioning loyalty to the sovereign, a duty which, together with its corollary, *noblesse oblige,* is in fact as well as in theory the moral foundation of nobility.

The Cornelian lessons of his father's reminiscences were an accompaniment to strict practical discipline exerted by Mme de Vigny. This lady was an articulate and severe rationalist (and professing Christian) in the grand style of the eighteenth century. She saw to it that her son's inherited feudal obligations would be carried out by a man well trained physically, mentally, and morally according to the prescriptions of Jean-Jacques Rousseau. If her religious indoctrination was expressed in Voltairian terminology, she also remembered that orthodox gestures are required of a nobleman. If she made Vigny learn his catechism, she also (exceptionally) provided him with a Bible.

At the proper age, Vigny was sent out of the house for formal education. He attended two schools, both of them as a day student, probably for financial reasons. One of them was the Pension Hix (1807–11); the other was the lycée variously known as Bonaparte, Bourbon, and now Condorcet. He disliked both of them intensely—mostly, it appears, because he lacked the physical equipment successfully to defend against his Republican and Bonapartist schoolmates the honor of the Bourbon nobility to which he so proudly belonged. He left the lycée to become sublieutenant in the First Regiment of the Gendarmes du Roi. This outfit, known also from its uniform as the Rouges, was an elite (i.e., ceremonial) corps assigned to guard the royal household; it was composed entirely of officers. Vigny joined it in July, 1814; in March, 1815 it escorted Louis XVIII and his family on their escape from what turned out to be merely the Hundred Days. Waterloo took place on June 18. The Rouges were disbanded on September 1, and Vigny transferred to the Garde Royale, another elite corps. This in turn was disbanded, and Vigny went to a line regiment of infantry, the 55th, in which he would remain until finally leaving the service as a captain in 1827. Apart from the flight from the Hundred Days, his sole warlike excitements consisted of duty on the Spanish frontier during the intervention in 1823, 1824, and 1825. Here, as everywhere else in his army career (Vincennes, Versailles, Rouen, Strasbourg, Bordeaux), he was on garrison duty. His dreams of a glory to be won in combat were never to be realized, and his letters and the journal show him suitably chafing at this frustration. He consoled himself by reading and writing, and by getting married. To facilitate these activities, he repeatedly sought and obtained leave. Between June, 1822 and his final separation from the service in April, 1827, he spent vastly more time on leave than on duty; indeed, he seems to have performed no active service at all after March 28, 1825.[3] Nobility's obligations were evidently not, in this era, to be fulfilled by the sword or by knightly prowess, but rather, however unfeudally, by pen and brain.

But these would not be the pen and the brain of an ordinary professional writer. Like many of his contemporaries, Vigny was outspokenly contemptuous of most journalists and publicists as being untalented hacks and the hirelings of faction.[4] The aristocrat of letters will necessarily be disinterested, penetrating, incorruptible; his insights will be exhibited for the service of king and country (though there is nothing in Vigny of either the court poet or the ostensibly fervent Catholic that was the early Hugo); his pen will give clear and striking expression to these distillations of truth. Mere entertainment and the autobiographical display of sentiment are not to be published by Vigny. A given work is to consist of a "Thought" (*Pensée*) fleshed out in some widely known story or image or character, carefully chosen and single-mindedly developed without the luxury of digression or the evocation of ancillary interests. All parts of the work will subserve directly the realization of its single intention. "Imagination gives body to ideas and creates for them living types and symbols which are so to speak the palpable form and the proof of an abstract theory. Thus philosophy can find weapons in this arsenal created by great men, and expressions and names which will give more clarity to the ideas." [5] It seems fair to say that, by and large, Vigny's works are intended to live up to this prescription. More purely and more consistently than those of most other writers, his poems, plays, and prose fiction are so many metaphors, so many organizations of symbols, in the service of ideas.

III *The Making of an Art*

1. *Prose*

The process of Vigny's fabrication of a satisfactory medium may most easily be seen in some details of two of his prose works, *Cinq-Mars* and *L'Alméh*. Considered as works of art, neither of them has very well stood the test of time. Their weakness results precisely from the fact that they are experimental, that they exemplify rather the search for a suitable instrument than the application of a perfected one. Let this be my excuse for some extensive quotations from them.

Cinq-Mars was written and published in 1826. *L'Alméh*, never finished, was apparently being written in 1828–29; it was published in the *Revue des deux mondes* in 1831. Because of its relatively raw state, it seems useful to examine *L'Alméh* before turning to *Cinq-Mars*.

L'Alméh was to be a historical novel, in the sense that its events were to be provoked by Napoleon Bonaparte's expedition to Egypt in 1798. The manner of its beginning belongs to the currently fashionable tradition of Sir Walter Scott. The conduct of its opening chapter is also remarkably similar to much of the first chapter of Cooper's *The Last of the Mohicans,* which is of 1826. Here is Vigny:

This story begins amid the peaceful, clear and cold nights of Said, the Arabic name for Upper Egypt, in the year of the hegira 1212, which Christians call the year 1797, and which the French then called the Year VI of the Republic, and in the desert which stretches out on the left bank of the Nile, a few leagues from the great ruins of Thebes. The light of the night was pure as it always is in that fair climate; but as the horizon there is continually veiled by light mists, it was only at the zenith that the big stars of the torrid zone and the constellations strange to the eye of the European could be seen. An uneven, whitish land, undulating like snow but without its sheen, stretched out to the horizon like an immense sheet whose sad monotony was broken by nothing. This kind of motionless sea had a wan, lustreless glow, and shadowless sands extended everywhere. Solitary in the midst of the empty, sterile land, there rose up two colossi, like two rocks in the ocean; these enormous figures, of unequal size, rested, seated side by side, upon thrones of black granite, big as two hills; by the starlight one could make out their immense arms resting on their joined knees; and high in the air gleamed their mutilated heads, which rose above their shoulders like two great towers upon two neighboring mountains. These ancient statues seemed to reign over the desert and impose upon it its silence: everything, even the air itself, was without movement, but sometimes a sudden, rapid breeze, coming from the Red Sea, drove flying before it a little of the fine sand of the plain; and then, as if this dead land had made a vain effort to shake itself and revive, everything fell again into an eternal rest.

But an unaccustomed sound rose suddenly in the silent night; it was a light tinkling of little bells, shaken by a frequent, regular movement; a whitish mass, running rapidly, approached the colossi and circled twice around them.

It was a little white elephant, of the smallest size, which went by at a rapid, loping trot: a man seemed to be seated on its back, in the midst of several raised bundles; twelve other men were running alongside the elephant; a child was lying on its head. Having gone around the statues, the elephant was stopped by its guide between the two colossi, near the base of the larger, which is sixty feet high; the elephant's trunk did not reach its foot. A small reddish light was shining on the sand; it illuminated the interior of an Arab tent set on four stakes and covered with goatskins. This nomad shelter was leaning against the immortal, heavy base of the statue of Memnon, and rose scarcely halfway up its pedestal. The joined feet of the colossus seemed like a double dome over the tent which they shaded. . . . The newcomer, having slid down the side of the kneeling elephant, and ordered it led some distance away by the men in his retinue, entered the tent alone.[6]

Therein the Brahman visitor finds three Arabs, an old man, a young man, and a young girl (the last, until his arrival, exotically bare-breasted). Gestures of greeting and hospitality having been made, the Indian pronounces a long speech in his language, which is unintelligible to his audience except for the word *Brahma*. The old Arab therefore sends the young one in search of a "Frank," who in the following chapter will be presented as a rather cynical Occidental, of unspecified nationality, to whom all languages are familiar.

It is clear that this introduction is inept from a number of points of view. Vigny had no real knowledge whatever of the scene and the objects which he here describes. His geography and his astronomy are uncertain, to say the least; even if we accept the "torrid zone" and its "strange constellations," the "sudden breeze" from the hundred-mile distant Red Sea seems unlikely. So too do the Brahman and his little white elephant, and the twelve companions who not only travel in the desert on foot, but are able to keep up with the fast-trotting beast. The year 1212 of the hegira was not 1797, but 1834. And so on.

It seems obvious, however, that for Vigny the objective accuracy or the likelihood of the ingredients of this scene is a matter of very small weight. What is important is their placement, their juxtaposition, the qualities, colors, sounds, effects, etc., that Vigny sees fit to give them, the ways in which he chooses to indite them. The year, for example, is 1797; we are told with emphasis that, while it is the same year for Moslem, Christian, and Republican (i.e., agnostic or atheist or heathen), each of these religionaries has his own way of designating it. We are told that the stars are very bright here; since the nights are always clear, the stars can be seen every night, but only by looking straight up; for as one's gaze comes down toward earth, one finds the horizon, the point where earth meets heaven, always obscured by mists. The lights of heaven are veiled, that is, by earth's emanations. It would be interesting, but surely not essential, to know how exact is Vigny's statement of Theban weather.

The prevailing whiteness of this landscape provides emphatic contrast with the objects at its center: the colossal statues on their black thrones, and the reddish-lit tent (whose covering goatskins may well be black). But there is so much whiteness in this passage that it seems probably intended to do more than furnish a contrasting background. The sand is "whitish, undulating like snow, but without its sheen"; this expanse has about it a "wan, lustreless glow"; the white sands are "shadowless"; the illumination is starlight; the horizon is veiled in mist; the breeze kicks up a little (white) sand. Even the elephant, which in its strangeness might well call for a contrasting color, is white. The whiteness in general is the more striking because it is seen at night.

The whiteness somehow belies itself because it neither shines nor casts nor bears shadows. The reality of the landscape belies its appearance. It looks like snow, but it is sand; it looks like an ocean, but it is dry and motionless. The elephant is real enough, but in its small size and its whiteness it does not look like most elephants. The desert and the elephant are solidly substantial, but in their whiteness there is no distinction, no particularization, no character.

So too for the colossi. They are huge and they are solid; they have lasted a very long time and will go right on lasting a very long time. But their heads are mutilated, in ruins; their knees and feet remain, doing nothing, however, to restore the identities which ruination has removed from their features.[7] Their durability, as objects, is quasi-eternal; their identity, their individuality, is frail and short-lived.

Against the whiteness and the immensity stands the small red and black object which is the illuminated tent, its frailty emphasized as it leans "against the immortal, heavy base of the statue." The tent and its occupants have some particularity, if not character, about them; they are Arab and Indian, Moslem and Hindu. They are set apart by their languages, among other things; the Brahman visitor, who has come for some serious, but unspecified, purpose, makes a long speech to his hosts "in the language of Hindustan, in which only the word *Brahma* was intelligible." The name of God is understood, but its pertinence in the visitor's oration is totally obscured by the rest of the foreign idiom. Communication here calls for interpretation, for an intermediary whose knowledge enables him to overcome the barriers imposed by localisms. We gather, as we read along, that the Interpreter was to have been the principal character of this novel.

The Interpreter is a European. Vigny prepares the introduction of him with some care, leading to it through the presentation of another European character. This latter is a Jesuit missionary who has adopted the name of Servus Dei. It seems appropriate to quote his description at some length.

The excellent man who had thought it appropriate to take this Latin name . . . had no doubt had another one in the world; but nothing has ever been known about it, and he always seemed to have completely forgotten it, never in his life having said a single word to indicate a remembrance of a way of life different from the one he was leading. He had installed himself in one of those large and splendid underground chambers of Thebes whose walls are covered with queer drawings and with hieroglyphics which are still very mysterious for us; this underground had its entrance in the immense tower of the palace of Medinet-Abu, which stands next to an old temple and a pavilion, former residence of Egyptian priests. Time had made him possessor of the outer and inner ruins of this gigantic building, with no trouble at all, since the miserable huts of the neighboring village were completely abandoned. The poor monk was thus the absolute master of one of the houses of the Pharaohs, and officiated in the sanctuary of the goddess Isis, being thus the spiritual and temporal sovereign of a palace beside which all the palaces of Rome and of all Europe would seem no more than smoky cottages or children's trinkets. Yet, however just may be the enthusiasm which leads us thus to point out the glory of our friend, we are bound to say that he was not the first religious conqueror of these magnificent abodes; they wore and still wear the traces of all the cults honored in Egypt: the Christians of the first Church of the Thebaid had raised a chapel in the court of the great temple; the Moslems then made a mosque of it, after purifying it with rose water; but time soon cast down this feeble building with its crosses and its crescents at the foot of the imperishable ruins [a lovely phrase!] which surrounded it like fortifications; there remained of it only some handsome columns of red granite, in one piece, which seem to be placed there as a point of comparison and scale between the narrow, paltry, and pretty taste of modern architecture, and the grandiose simplicity and the sublime beauty of ancient architecture and statuary.[8]

"Imperishable ruins": we are in the neighborhood of *Ozymandias of Egypt,* but the message is quite a different one. Ruins are worn by time, but they are made by men. These ruins, moreover, in their eternity have been used by a succession of men to carry a variety of meanings. Everlasting in substance, they have carried and continue to carry upon their surfaces the varying signs of successive formulations of men's notions of their relationships with eternity. In case his reader should have missed the point, Vigny becomes more specific:

The night in which took place the very simple events which we have to relate, was already far along, when Father Servus Dei emerged from his cellar, carrying a dark lantern in one hand and in the other a very heavy clay pot; he climbed up into the ruins, and, alone in the immense peristyle of the unroofed palace, he moved with sure steps towards the middle of the biggest wall, which was also the best preserved and the most thickly covered with drawings of battles and of religious ceremonies. There he stopped, and piling, not without difficulty, several stones upon one another, he made a sort of ladder, by means of which he mounted up level with a great figure of Osiris, seated on his victory car, holding in one hand the reins of his horses, and with the other making a sign of peace to a number of little men whose heads did not reach his knee, and who were spreading as an offering, under his chariot wheels, a rain of hands and ears cut off from his enemies. The good father, having set down his lantern beside him, began to consider the profile of Osiris . . . as a painter would look at a bad picture which he was supposed to improve; in silence he examined for some time the figure of the hawk which formed the headdress of the divine personage, and giving a soft sigh, he stood for a moment with his arms folded, attentively considering it. Finally, suddenly making up his mind, he dipped a brush into the pot that he had brought and rotated it a long time, and, pulling it out all swollen with beautiful yellow ochre paint, applied it to the wall, and drew a half circle around the head of Osiris; then, being extremely careful to bring the profile out sharply, and to conceal the head of the hawk, he filled in the circumference with his pasty paint so as to form a sort of moon behind the head and shoulders of the ex-

Egyptian god. Very satisfied with his work, he came down from his stone ladder to examine it from a distance, cocked his bald head to the right and then to the left, and stroked his grey-bearded chin with the air of a consummate artist; then, remounting his scaffolding, and grasping again his big brush, he was preparing to correct the extended hand of the god, when a loud voice made the echoes of the peristyle resound with a long, ironical burst of laughter, which startled the good missionary; he turned his head in some embarrassment, and saw at the base of his pedestal a man whose presence caused him no surprise, but a slight movement of annoyance.[9]

It is the Interpreter who laughs. His amusement is founded upon solid and articulate skepticism, which in turn is based upon knowledge, and compounded with a sort of pity that he feels for the futility of the old man's activities. The Jesuit's annoyance arises from a sense of outrage at this disrespect for the signs of his religion, together with the hurt that one feels when a person whom one likes seems guilty of some reprehensible action. For, despite his kindliness and his timidity, the missionary is a rigorist, the more so, no doubt, because of the difficulties and the compromises which have been forced upon him for so long. Of the many revised decorations upon the temple walls, his favorite is one which had been "an Ozymandias trampling upon two Ethiopians; but as he had been made over into a Saint Peter crushing Eutyches and Nestorius, the founders of the schism which bears their name, this was the painting which commanded the most devoted contemplation of our pious hero." [10] Father Servus Dei is a Roman Catholic to the letter, intolerant of deviation in either doctrine or gesture, and conscience-struck at the concessions he himself has made under duress. He is a devout believer in signs, in icons, in gestures and ceremonials, in all the outward evidences which presumably manifest the true faith. No one knows better than he the superficiality and the exiguity of these things; yet no one more consistently than he attempts to provide them, and this at the risk of death, either from the Mamelukes or from falling from his rickety perch. The Interpreter's laughter, to say nothing of his ways of thinking, is repulsive to the Jesuit; yet despite his rigorism, he feels deep affection for the younger man.

"You know," he says to him, "that I already love you as a son, although I don't know who you are." [11] The Interpreter's activities, like his origin, his nationality, his circumstances, are mysterious, and the priest is troubled by the mystery surrounding "a young man who interested him intensely and inspired in him a compassion which suspicions could not destroy." [12] In spite of the skeptic's deplorable principles and possible criminality, the old man "felt a great inclination to like him, although he had found in him a habitual irony of speech which had in it something cold, desperate, and sinister, and a taste for sophism which made of all his conversations so many arguments at the bottom of which his true opinion was as impenetrable as was the place of his birth." [13] It is true that the Interpreter seems to be a Frenchman, that he is educated and civilized, that, aside from the priest's late colleague Father Felix, he is the only person to whom Father Servus Dei has felt able to open his mind and his confidence in the past forty years. The confidence is nonetheless incomplete, and the missionary puzzles over the situation. "The outcome of the good monk's reflections was that at which many other men have arrived . . . when they have sought to sound the hearts of those who surrounded them. His conclusion was that he did not have a friend." [14] Yet he cannot escape being drawn to the young man.

The latter is, or should be, a familiar figure to us, if not to the Jesuit. His face is "noble and expressive"; "his hollow, burning eyes were full of unquiet thought; he was blond, and his tanned complexion, like that of seamen, seemed intended to be whiter, judging from the lighter color of his hands and his neck." His costume is blue in color;[15] like his other accoutrements, it is of indeterminate nationality. "The whole of his person had about it something European and Asiatic at the same time which gave a fair idea of the double nature of an interpreter." His hands are "muscular and spare." He speaks an unspecified number of languages, all of them fluently, and apparently, like his French, without accent. For all his youth, he has been in far places, including India, and seen many strange things. "His grave character and the great breadth of his knowledge . . . had procured for him from the moment of his arrival an almost superstitious veneration on the part of the sheiks and all the region, where he had come to live only six months previously."

According to him, his character and personality are as grim as his career is mysterious. Father Servus Dei having complained that he does not know who the young man is, the latter replies:

God grant, Father, that I be unknown to everyone. I and those like me must wish only for that destiny. But the time is going to come when I should encounter many dangers, if there were dangers for a man who, at bottom, cares nothing for what will become of him. . . .I am eternally on a journey; my stay here was only an interruption. . . . I cannot name to you those who are coming [he refers to the French invasion; his reluctance to name the invaders is inexplicable, the more so because he states both names and numbers in the following chapter], but they will make themselves clearly seen and heard; and I tell you on my honor, when they come, there will not be one hair of my head in safety.[16]

The priest having said that those are at peace whose conscience is clear: "There! there are the suspicions that I shall always inspire, and you can't help having them . . . but that's all right with me. . . . The opinion of men does not concern me. What difference does it make to me?" This, adds Vigny, "was his favorite phrase." [17]

Our man is not only a mysterious, solitary, eternally wandering misanthrope who believes himself to be important enough to be persecuted; it seems that he is also dangerous to know, and sufficiently generous to try to avoid bringing misfortune upon those who innocently associate with him. To the priest, who is increasingly bothered by his mystery, he speaks in a sudden burst of half-confidence:

"Please believe, good Father, that I am not amusing myself by tormenting you with vain predictions, and that if I still keep secret my name and my country, it is less for my sake than for yours, for in the eyes of those whose arrival I am expecting, you would be just as compromised as I am. Just as guilty," he added with a scornful laugh, "just as guilty of *lèse-nation*. Ha! ha! you will soon learn what that crime is. I am telling you enough, Father, so that later on you may guess at what I am, when you are better informed of the most recent events in Europe; but I shall make you no confidence which might compromise or commit you, I ask no promise of you. Suppress nothing of what I have said, mention your suspicions to whom you will, I have no right to demand anything of you. You are free; we shall see what you will do." [18]

Since the priest could presumably endanger himself merely by admitting to having associated with the Interpreter, the latter's generosity here seems a bit fatuous. In terms of plot, at any rate, it is now plain that our man is a Frenchman who has seen the Revolution, has been on the monarchist, or losing, side of it, has escaped to foreign parts, and is now disturbed by the present arrival in his Egyptian neighborhood of the Revolution's formidable favorite child, Napoleon.

More interesting for us is the fact that the figure here described, in its mystery, its misanthropy, its skepticism, its vague allegations of criminality, its homelessness, its wide experience and great knowledge, its seemingly irresistible but nefarious charm, and (not least) its rather childish fatuity—this figure is no less (or more) than another of the myriad Romantic heroes according to the recipes of Chateaubriand and Byron. Like many of those others too, it is, or would have been, something of a self-portrait. At the very least, the Interpreter is like Vigny in being blond, spare, grave, aloof, monarchist, and disillusioned.

There is indeed yet more to the resemblance. To the stuff of Manfred and René have been added two important particularizing elements. The Interpreter is going to be a man of definite, positive action. And so is Napoleon. And the action will serve an idea clearly understood and clearly expressed to the reader. We do not know, of course, how the action was to be worked out. But the idea seems obvious enough. No religion, no matter what its doctrines, forms, venerability, no matter how dedicated its minions, can fulfill the function for which religions are formed: the procurement of the well-being of mankind. This end can be achieved only when leaders and people alike recognize the fundamental sameness of all men everywhere, bend their efforts to the objective and complete study of man's nature, and construct upon this scientific, physical basis a single, worldwide civilization. The first step in this procedure must be to expose the falsehood, inefficacy, emptiness, wrongness of existing institutions and traditions. Thus most of the text of *L'Alméh* presents the spectacle, in symbol and in discourse, of what Bonnefoy calls the deterioration of religions.[19]

The deterioration will inevitably take place with the passage of time. It can be speeded, on occasion, as Vigny's Jesuit sadly visualizes, by "those great invasions by which, from time to time, one people hurls itself upon another, one race crushes another, effaces its religious and human laws, reduces its language to silence and makes of it a dead science, and covers up the preceding civilization with all the weight of its own, as a layer of earth, suddenly caved in, allows but a few trees and a few large buildings to show their tops [amidst] the remade landscape." [20] But the old invasions have merely substituted one set of temporary institutions and superstitions for another. This time, perhaps, with the clear-sighted, unprejudiced guidance of a pure intellect nourished by vast and exact knowledge, coupled with powerful and decisive action, a start might be made at last on the proper path to the desired millennium. It seems not unlikely that Vigny intended some such coupling to take place in his novel between the Interpreter and Napoleon.

In any case, the notion of the successive imposition of different religious traditions upon the unchanging, constant matter of humanity is amply (I should say too amply) symbolized in the pages that I have quoted and more besides. The work is overdone; the obvious is very soundly belabored. But it seems worth attention for just that reason, because it betrays Vigny's overmastering preoccupation with the desire to symbolize, to clothe the idea in substance and, by manipulating the substance, to display the many lights and facets of the idea.

L'Alméh's technique, crude and exaggerated as it is, is yet more flexible and subtle than that of the earlier *Cinq-Mars*. Vigny's means here are primarily persons who, being historical and (most of them) historically prominent, perform symbolic functions merely by being mentioned. Since its publication, *Cinq-Mars* has often been criticized for the woodenness of its characters, especially that of Richelieu, and the criticism is justified. It should also be said, however, on the one hand that it is unfair to dismiss these characters simply as being lay figures; stiff they are, without any doubt, but they are by no means quite devoid of life. At the same time, Vigny expressly intended his characters to represent ideas and principles, and it is with some surprise that we notice a spark of life in some of them.

The plot of *Cinq-Mars* is soon told. Its protagonist is the young Henri d'Effiat, marquis de Cinq-Mars, who in fact became a favorite of Louis XIII, took part in a conspiracy against Richelieu's efforts to concentrate all power in the throne, and was beheaded for his pains in 1642 at the age of twenty-two. Vigny

makes of his hero the leader of the conspiracy and attributes
its failure to Cinq-Mars' substitution of personal ambition for
clear-headed devotion to the cause. We are shown the young
man leaving for the first time the bosom of his family to join
king, cardinal, and royal forces at Narbonne. On the way he
passes through Loudun at the proper time to witness the trial
and execution of Urbain Grandier, convicted of witchcraft; his
real crime is of course his opposition to Richelieu. Thus
instructed and outraged, our hero joins the army, is presented
to the king, learns something about protocol and politics, distinguishes himself in a skirmish or two, and continues discreetly
to nurse a profound distaste for the cardinal. The scene shifts
abruptly to Paris, where we find him installed as the king's
reigning favorite, and consequently the focal point for court
intrigue. Much of the nobility is quite justifiably hostile to
Richelieu. Cinq-Mars sets out to lead a conspiracy, whose nom-
inal head is the king's pusillanimous brother, the duc d'Orleans.
The objective is Richelieu's overthrow; it is Cinq-Mars' ambition
to take the cardinal's place as chief minister. One of his problems
is to reconcile his conspiratorial activity with his absolute loyalty to the throne; the difficulty is complicated by the fact that,
in order to succeed, the plot must use armed foreign (Spanish)
intervention. Another arises from his growing awareness that the
source of his ambition is not loyalty to king and country so much
as it is his love for Marie de Gonzague, Duchess of Mantua, a
royal princess betrothed to the king of Poland. To win her,
Cinq-Mars must achieve quasi-royalty for himself. This problem too has its complication: Marie is a dear, sweet girl, but
her passion for Cinq-Mars is tepid and fickle. It goes without
saying that all calculations are forestalled and ruled by Richelieu, abetted by an incredibly rascally Father Joseph, the Grey
Eminence. What with Richelieu's sagacity, the moral and intellectual weakness of Louis XIII, and his own impulsiveness,
Cinq-Mars shortly finds himself in Lyon with his neck on the
block, and Marie de Gonzague is the momentarily tearful queen
of Poland.

This plot line, such as it is, is dictated by history. Vigny puts
it to work to illustrate a thesis: namely, that the strength and
happiness of a people are best assured by an ideal feudal regime,
a divine-right monarch loyally supported by a virtuous and

powerful nobility. The illustration is negative; we are to understand that Richelieu's emasculation of the nobility has resulted in misery and disaster for the nation. We see further that the triumph of Richelieu is that of objective intellect over sentiment and passion.

The first of these propositions is, in Vigny's view, at least, historical fact. As such it belongs to the category of phenomena which he entitles "le Vrai"—the True. The second proposition implies an understanding in detail of the various ways in which the faculties and the psychological characteristics of the participants operate to produce *le Vrai*. These operations, the conglomeration, that is, of the human impulsions, reasoned and otherwise, which make the facts to be as they are, Vigny calls "la Vérité"—the Truth.

He does this in the theoretical disquisition, *Réflexions sur la vérité dans l'art,* which he wrote in 1827 and appended as a preface to *Cinq-Mars.* According to this document, it is the task of history to record *le Vrai,* while the historical novel exhibits *la Vérité,* supplying what might be called the human explanation of historical events. Looking within himself, says Vigny, man finds "two needs which seem opposed, but which are mingled, as I see it, in a common source: one is the love of the true, the other the love of the fictional [*fabuleux*]. The day when Man first narrated his life to Man, History was born. But of what use is the memory of true facts, if not to exemplify good or evil?" [21] The totality of facts, of human actions, he goes on, no doubt forms a pattern, but it is one too vast to be perceived by any eye but God's. All philosophies have tried, none of them successfully, to explain it.

Thus it seems to me that man, having satisfied his first curiosity for facts, desired something more complete, some grouping, some reduction to his own scale and use, of the links of that vast chain of events which his view could not comprehend; for he also wished to find, in the narrations, examples which might serve for the moral truths of which he was aware; few individual destinies were sufficient for this desire, being only incomplete parts of the incomprehensible Whole of the history of the world; one was so to speak the quarter, the other the half, of a proof; imagination did the rest and completed them. This, no doubt, was the origin of fiction.— Man created it true, because it is not given to him to see anything other than himself and the nature which surrounds him; but he created it True *[Vraie]* with an altogether peculiar Truth *[Vérité].*[22]

Fiction is smaller than history, being the choice of exemplary fragments, these to be imaginatively completed. This last clause is pregnant of a great deal. "This Truth, altogether beautiful, altogether intellectual, which I feel, which I see and wish to define . . . is as it were the soul of all the arts. It is a choice of the characteristic sign from among all the beauties and all the grandeurs of the visible True." And then comes Vigny's statement of a theory of the dignity of art which has been held by some in all times, but never more generally nor more explicitly than in nineteenth-century France:

But [the chosen, characteristic sign of the visible True] is not the True itself, it is better than the True; it is an ideal grouping *[ensemble]* of its principal forms, a luminous hue composed of its liveliest colors, an intoxicating balsam made of its purest odors, a delicious elixir of its best juices, a perfect harmony of its most melodious sounds; in a word, it is a sum total of all its values. Dramatic works, those works of Art which are a moral representation of life, must aspire to this Truth alone. In order to reach it, one must no doubt begin by knowing all of the True of each age, by being deeply imbued with its whole and its parts; [this accomplishment calls merely for] attention, patience, and memory; but then one must choose and group [one's choices] about an invented center; this is the work of the imagination and of that great Common Sense which is genius itself.[23]

Fiction, it seems, is truer than history. The novelist appears to be ranked above the historian, whose task is performed by "attention, patience, and memory," without requiring the intervention of imagination or genius. By the same token, the materials provided by history—such things as dates, geographical locations, costumes, manners, the actual appearance and character of specific persons—need command no particular respect on the part of the novelist. Historical realism is a very minor virtue in a work of art. "What good would the Arts be if they were simply the reproduction, the copy, of existence?"[24] On the contrary, Vigny believes that one should give little importance to

historical reality in judging dramatic works, poems, novels, or tragedies which borrow memorable characters from history. Art must never be considered otherwise than in its relationships with its Ideal Beauty. We are forced to say it: what is True is only secondary; it is only an additional illusion with which [Art] embellishes itself, one of our inclinations which it flatters. [Art] could get along without it [the True], for the Truth which must nourish it is *the truth of observation upon human nature,* and not *the authenticity of the fact.* The names of the characters are of no importance to the thing.

The Idea is everything. The proper name is nothing but the example and the proof of the idea.[25]

Perhaps the most obvious thing about this passage, apart from the sloppiness of its writing, is its attempt to answer critics of *Cinq-Mars* who have been scolding Vigny for playing fast and loose with historical data. And so he has done. The sin becomes spectacular in one chapter (XX), in which he brings together on one evening in 1641 or 1642, and under one roof, a list of persons which sounds somewhat like a set of chapter headings from a history of seventeenth-century literature. In the house of Marion de Lorme, we are told, are assembled among others the following: Desbarreaux, Baro, Gombauld, Colletet, Pierre Corneille, Molière, John Milton, Georges de Scudéry, Vaugelas, Godeau, Descartes, Ninon de Lenclos, and Gondi, the future Cardinal de Retz. These are there in addition to the hostess, Cinq-Mars, his faithful friend de Thou, and an assortment of more or less remembered noblemen and soldiers. Quite apart from various chronological impossibilities, the credibility of this gathering is simply nonexistent, and Vigny certainly needed no critic to tell him so. It therefore seems likely that in stating that "the proper name is nothing but the example and proof of the idea," he is not engaging in an *ex post facto* defense of his own ineptitude, but rather formulating a principle which he has conscientiously thought out and put into practice.

In the present instance, his list of literati is made up not at all with an eye to historical verisimilitude, but rather to indicate, with a succinctness he could scarcely have obtained in any other way, the composition and the complexity of the intellectual atmosphere in which on this night the conspiracy will be hatched. Vigny divides his writers into two categories, even as do histories of literature. The first and larger is that of the *précieux* and the academicians: Vaugelas, Gombauld, Baro,

Scudéry, Godeau, Desbarreaux, and Retz. These represent the authority of current fashionable taste, and for Vigny this taste is false. The remainder, Corneille, Molière, Descartes, and Milton are true poets and thinkers, in the sense that their judgment is unhampered by the demands of fashion and academic prescription, and their works have survived a succession of changing authorities. Milton is made to read to the assembly some portions of *Paradise Lost*; he is interrupted by a footman's shouted announcement of arriving guests. "The listeners took advantage of [the interruption] to start a dozen separate conversations"; almost without exception the comments consist of

. . . words of blame and accusations of bad taste; a few men of wit, numbed by routine, exclaimed that they did not understand, that it was above their intelligence (little thinking that they spoke so true) and, by this false humility, they acquired for themselves a compliment, and for the poet an insult: a double advantage. A few even pronounced the word *profanation*. The interrupted poet put his head in his hands and his elbows on the table, in order not to hear all this noise of politeness and criticism. Only three men came to him: an officer [Descartes], Poquelin [Molière] and Corneille; the latter whispered in Milton's ear: "I advise you to change to a different passage; your audience is not up to the level of this one." The officer shook the English poet's hand and said: "I admire you with all the strength of my soul." The Englishman looked at him in surprise and saw a face which was intelligent, passionate, and ill.[26]

While Desbarreaux, Godeau, Scudéry, and Baro are giving their disapproval its properly euphuistic expression, the four men of authentic genius are joined by de Thou, the noble, intelligent, and generous friend of Cinq-Mars; having been introduced to Descartes, he "smiled with pleasure on hearing the simple language of the superior man, the language that he loved best after that of friendship; he shook hands with the young sage from Touraine and drew him into a neighboring room together with Corneille, Milton, and Molière, and there they had the kind of conversation which makes the time which precedes and follows it seem wasted."[27]

The point of this scene in a literary *salon* seems to be to identify de Thou with the authentic poetic-prophetic genius which finds in itself, and without regard for contemporary fashion, the sole authority for the creation and judgment of works whose excellence, speaking to all perceptive men everywhere, is impervious to the passage of history. The presentation of the writers here, *précieux* and men of genius alike, seems exaggerated, overdone, like the art work of Father Servus Dei, but this very exaggeration again makes obvious the symbolic nature of Vigny's intentions. It is unnecessary, and also laughable, at least for a French audience, to make Scudéry (in 1642) give (as Vigny makes him do) a detailed account of the famous *carte du tendre* in his sister's *Clélie,* which was published between 1654 and 1660; it is ridiculous to show young Molière (twenty years old in 1642), rebuffed by the same Scudéry, "consoling himself by pondering the *Précieuses ridicules*" of 1659. Such lapses, not so much from taste as from chronology and common sense, presumably imply strong motivation on the part of an author as self-conscious as Vigny was. And in the case of this chapter, and of the novel as a whole, it seems clear that Vigny is inordinately preoccupied with a technique of altering historical personages into symbols.

Let us not attribute this to Vigny's ignorance of history. *Cinq-Mars,* like most of his other works, is as meticulously researched as anyone could wish. When his king, his cardinal, his priests, poets, courtesans, and so on are altered from their historical selves, the deformation has taken place with the full knowledge and thus, we infer, with the deliberate intention of the author. Almost inevitably there results the making of puppet-characters, a completely cynical Richelieu, a completely villainous Father Joseph, a completely selfless de Thou, a completely right Urbain Grandier, a completely vacillating Louis XIII. Vigny is aware of the danger and tries, with middling success, to obviate it, at least in some of the principal characters: the king, the cardinal, and Cinq-Mars.

But his means in this endeavor tend to be more discursive than substantial; I mean that he accomplishes it for the most part only by telling us, or having the character tell us, that he is not altogether a puppet, that there are moments when his unity breaks down. So, for example, in the case of Richelieu, who, having exhibited his inexorable cynicism and decisiveness to Father Joseph (Chapter XXII), finds himself alone, weary, and spitting blood. He makes a rather long soliloquy, which terminates as follows:

Great God, if you hear me, then judge me, but do not isolate me in order to judge me. Look upon me surrounded by the men of my century; look upon the immense work that I had undertaken; could these masses be moved by anything less than an enormous lever? and if that lever crushes a few useless wretches as it falls, am I very guilty? To men I shall seem evil; but you, supreme judge, will you see me so? No; you know what the limitless power is which makes the creature guilty towards the creature; it is not Armand de Richelieu who brings death, it is the prime minister. It is not for personal injuries, but for the sake of following out a system. But a system . . . what is this word? Was it permitted me thus to play with men, and to look upon them as though they were ciphers in order to realize a thought, a false thought, perhaps? I am overturning the entourage of the throne. Suppose, without knowing it, that I were really undermining its foundations and hastening its fall! Yes, my borrowed power has seduced me. Oh labyrinth! oh weakness of human thought! . . . Simple faith, why did I leave your path? . . . why am I not merely a simple priest? If I dared break with man and give myself to God, Jacob's ladder would again come down in my dreams![28]

This is oratory pure and also simple. Nothing in the actions or the fabric of this character shows the foregoing speech to be of any consequence. The character is in no sense the human being Armand Duplessis, or any other human being, but only the sign and symbol of the ruthless policy of destituting the power of the nobility of France in favor of the throne.

Sign and symbol too is the wavering, faltering figure of Louis XIII. The novel's thesis would have it that the destruction of the nobility was at last the responsibility of the monarch, who had, after all, the God-given authority to prevent, by saying the right word at the appropriate time, the annihilation of the force which had raised up the throne. Vigny blames the situation on the shortsightedness, ineptitude, and cowardice of the Bourbons. It may well be that because Louis VIII must embody these deficiencies his characterization is the most nearly human one in the book.

Our first searching view of the king takes place in an interview with Cinq-Mars at the château of Chambord. Vigny introduces the conversation with the most dazzling piece of symbolic description in the work.

Four leagues from Blois, an hour from the Loire, in a very low little valley, between the muddy swamps and a forest of big oaks, far from all roads, one suddenly comes upon a royal, or rather, magic château. You would say that, compelled by some miraculous lamp, an oriental genie had picked it up during one of the thousand nights and stolen it away from the land of the Sun, to hide it in the land of the mist with the loves of a handsome prince. This palace is buried like a treasure; but, at sight of its blue domes, its elegant minarets, rounded above broad walls or thrust up in the air, at sight of its long terraces overlooking the woods, its delicate spires swayed by the wind, its crescents interlaced everywhere on its colonnades, one would think himself in the kingdom of Bagdad or Kashmir, if the blackened walls, with their coverings of moss or vines, and the pale, melancholy color of the sky, did not reveal a rainy country. It was indeed a genie [in French a pun on *genius*] who raised these structures, but he came from Italy and was called Primaticcio; it was indeed a handsome prince whose loves were hidden there, but he was a king and his name was Francis the First. IIis salamander spouts its flames everywhere there; it sparkles a thousand times repeated on the vaults, and multiplies its flames on them like the stars in a sky; it holds up the capitals with its burning crown; it colors the stained glass with its fires; it winds like a serpent along the secret stairways and, everywhere, seems to devour with its flaming eyes the triple crescents of a mysterious Diana, that Diane de Poitiers, twice goddess and twice worshipped in this voluptuous forest.[29]

The prince who built this palace was indeed a king after the heart of Vigny, who chooses not to mention that Francis I was Valois and not Bourbon, and also went to defeat at the hands of Charles V. Of the palace, at least, there is no doubt, and if Vigny describes it in terms of *Arabian Nights* magic, he has his reasons.

For the real and flabby prince presently inhabiting Chambord is trying by his choice to live in a fairy tale, to hide from reality, the ugly reality that, while he has the name of king, the fact of kingship resides elsewhere; this, and the even more agonizing reality that he need only decide and speak in order to place the kingship where he will. Decision he cannot face; and so, in his magic palace, he shelters himself by preference in its most peculiar apartment.

The base [sic] of this strange monument is, like the rest of it, full of elegance and mystery: it is a double staircase which rises in two interlaced spirals up from the building's lowest foundations to above

its highest belfries, and terminates in a lantern-turret, or open chamber, crowned with a colossal fleur-de-lis, which can be seen from a
long way off; two men can climb it at the same time without seeing
each other.

This stairway itself seems to be a small, isolated temple; like our
churches, it is supported and protected by the arches of its wings,
which are thin, transparent, and so to speak embroidered with open
work. One would think that the docile stone had made itself flexible
under the finger of the architect; it seems molded according to the
caprices of his imagination. It is difficult to conceive how the plans
for it were drawn and in what terms the orders were explained to
the workmen; the structure seems like a fleeting thought, a brilliant daydream which has suddenly taken on a durable body. It is
a dream come true.[30]

At the summit of this temple hides the king.

One's ascent to the royal presence is not a straight path, but
the pursuit of a continuous curve; it is moreover possible to be
accompanied or passed in this access without knowing the
identity or even the presence of one's fellow travelers. Cinq-Mars
mounts the spiral (Chapter XIX) for a private interview with
the king, in the course of which he comes as close as he ever will
to assuring the success of his great design. Louis displays his
customary indecision, giving outlandish importance to trivialities
and personal pique, shying away from the affair that really matters, and finally dismissing Cinq-Mars: "You may speak to your
friends about it, and I will give it serious thought." Cinq-Mars'
descent of the staircase begins his descent to his doom; as he
starts down, he is aware that someone else is coming up the
other spiral. This later turns out to have been Father Joseph,
Richelieu's representative and the most important part of the
mechanism of Cinq-Mars' downfall.

Such symbolism as this is primitive and crude; Vigny in this
book relies much more upon discursive, analytical procedure.
Even in the novel's climactic chapter (XXIV), where Richelieu
dares the king to rule for himself, and Louis rapidly gets hope-
lessly lost in the files of diplomatic dispatches, the treatment is
only momentarily and exceptionally symbolic, and the symbolism
remains gross. The fainting Louis having recalled the cardinal
in despair at his own helplessness, Richelieu appears beside him
like "a doctor at his patient's bedside."

"You called me back," said he, "what do you want of me?" Louis, lying back upon his pillow, half opened his eyes and looked at him, and then shut them hastily. The fleshless head, with its flaming eyes and pointed, whitish beard, the skullcap and the garments of the color of blood and flames, everything betokened to him a spirit from Hell. "Reign," he said in a weak voice.[31]

Richelieu consents, in return for the heads of Cinq-Mars and de Thou, and the custody of the king's own sons as hostages. And the representation of Richelieu as Satan is obvious, and its intended function is obvious, and the whole thing seems somehow too easy.

All the same, this chapter does not present Richelieu simply as evil incarnate. The cardinal is an antagonist, to be sure; the cause he serves is indeed wrong from the point of view of this novel. It is not, however, evil that he incarnates, but intellect— intellect free of any taint or tinge of feeling. The use of *esprit* in the passage just quoted ("a spirit from Hell—*un esprit infernal*") is a punning one: "infernal mind" as well as "infernal spirit." Satan, Lucifer, the Angel of Light, is the patron of the mind, the intellectual faculty of death and damnation, the fatal talent without which no human action can succeed; by the same token, successful action is accursed of God (and of the righteous). The project of Cinq-Mars must fail, not because of its essential rightness or wrongness, but because it is conceived in passion and passionately pursued.

The ideological scheme of *Cinq-Mars* is consistent with the belief that underlies all of Vigny's subsequent work: that the dignity of man and his actions must originate in the exercise of his intellect—that faculty which distinguishes him from all other creatures, and which he holds to in defiance of or (later) in the silence of God. Vigny's problem as an artist, to find appropriate metaphorical expressions for this scheme, is far from solved in *Cinq-Mars* and *L'Alméh*. For his temperament and his time, verse poetry seems on the face of it to provide a more manageable medium.

2. Poèmes Antiques et Modernes

It has already been said that from the beginning of his career, Vigny visualizes the poet in the role of prophet, seer, and inter-

preter of the highest truth. Thus he is always preoccupied with
the problem of man's relationships with higher things, and with
the existence and the nature of higher things. In 1822 he published his first book, *Poèmes,* a collection of ten pieces, including
Héléna. Of the remaining nine, we may dismiss five, *La Dryade,
Symétha, Le Somnambule, Le Bain,* and *Le Bal,* as being either
exercises in a traditional genre (e.g., *Dryade*: "Idyl after the
manner of Theocritus"), or displays of a more or less sensual
and picturesque ingenuity (*Somnambule, Bain*), or a routine
variation on a traditional theme (*Bal–"carpe diem"*). *Le Mal-
heur* is more interesting; it is an ode to spleen, camped squarely
in the notion of the *mal du siècle,* to be sure, but at same time
strikingly prefiguring Baudelaire. The other three, *La Fille de
Jephté* (1820), *La Femme adultère* (1819), and *La Prison*
(1821), interest us here because they present some views of the
nature of divinity.

If we believe Vigny's dating,[32] the earliest of the three is *La
Femme adultère* (152 lines). The climax of the poem recounts
the behavior of Jesus in the episode of the woman taken in
adultery. It is preceded by three short scenes: the adultery
itself, put together mostly out of the seventh chapter of Proverbs
and the "Song of Solomon";[33] the woman's next-morning remorse
for her wilful sin; her innocent merchant-husband, away on a
journey and looking forward to a happy homecoming. The
Jesus of the fourth part is unaltered in either character or
behavior from that of St. John's narration (8:3–9), but Vigny
terminates his poem with the dispersal of the crowd; he says
nothing of Jesus' refusal to condemn the woman. Her role in
this part is confined to weeping and raising her eyes to heaven,
except that as she stands before Jesus in the midst of the threat-
ening crowd, "her eyes seemed to be looking for someone else
as well." [34] The someone else is presumably her lover; in any
case, the line describes a divergent detail in a picture customarily so composed as to make the figure of Jesus its single
center. Jesus is the center of Vigny's picture for everyone, it
seems, except the woman, who would thus appear either unrepentant or vengeful (she looks for her lover, either hoping that
he may help her, or thinking that he should share her punishment). The crowd proclaims that he is dead; it is only then
that she is said to weep. At this point Jesus pronounces his cel-

ebrated judgment and resumes writing upon the sand as the people disperse. He looks up to find himself alone as the poem ends, and there is no further mention of the woman. The effect of all this is to separate the story of the woman from the story of the judgment. Vigny gives no sign that the woman is really aware of Jesus; on the contrary, she is as isolated from him as she is from the crowd.

One might attribute this situation to accident or to bad composition. But Vigny seems to have made it deliberately, and prepared it carefully in the second part of his poem. There he shows his heroine remorseful and frightened: "The first dawn is her first punishment. She saw her sin and her surroundings together. She was amazed at herself, and doubted her God. She joined her hands," as though in prayer, but her eyes betray her true thought as they remain fixed on the door through which her lover has gone out.[35] She seems as if dead; only her tears show that she is alive and sorrowing, but the causes of the sorrow are unspecified. There follows an extended simile,[36] comparing our heroine to Lot's wife escaping from Sodom. Of the latter, Gen. 19:26 tells us only that "she looked back [we do not know why], and she became a pillar of salt." But Vigny would have it that, "defying the celestial prohibition, she wanted once more to see the place of her childhood, or perhaps, listening to her ambitious heart, [she wanted] with a glance to detect [*surprendre*] the great secret of the heavens."[37] Vigny's wife of Lot is thus another seeker after forbidden knowledge, another Eve, and so, thanks to the simile and its sequel in the scene with Jesus, must be his adulterous woman. If her remorse is quickened by the arrival of her small son, it is mostly because in the child she sees her husband "returning to frighten her."[38] She knows, that is, the torments of a bad conscience; it is still a fact that we last see her weeping at the news of her lover's death. We conclude that Vigny's unrepentant Sephora, guilty and justly condemned under the law dictated to Moses by Jehovah, has gone unpunished thanks to Jesus' pity; "he, born in sorrows, king of the unfortunate,"[39] has come between the convicted sinner and Jehovah.

This poem presents two possible divinities. One is Jesus. He is called savior of the afflicted, the old, the children, the poor; he is fertile in miracles and gifted with prophecy; his disciples learn in a divine school, and he wears divine fires upon his serious brow; he is the Son of Man, who judges in the case, and whose mysterious finger writes a language strange to earth but known in heaven. By none of these characteristics is he associated with the fierce destroyer of Sodom, the capricious executioner of Lot's wife, who decreed also the lapidation of the adulteress. None of them, indeed, specifically asserts his divinity. But if this Jesus is to be considered a god, then he is clearly opposed to the other god, Jehovah.

The latter's character can also be seen in Vigny's treatment of the story of Jephthah.[40] Once again, he remains so faithful to his source in Judges 11–12 as to seem to be furnishing us with little more than a versified transcription. The poem begins and ends with the line: "This is what was sung by the daughters of Israel." [41] Jephté has conquered his enemies for the Lord; Israel knows it and is celebrating, "recognizing the all-powerful succour of the Most High." And Jephté is returning, "a sombre victor, walking with lowered head, deaf to the noise of glory, alone, silent; suddenly he stops, he has closed his eyes. He has closed his eyes, for afar, the virgins, singing, were coming from the town, slowly, calmly; he glimpses the pious choir; this is why, full of fear, he has closed his eyes." [42] The celebration in his honor continues to approach; he recognizes his daughter's voice, and she comes and embraces him, sees his gloom, and asks the reason; "has not the Lord overturned cities at the mere sound of your steps?" [43] Jephté explains: "Lord, you are indeed the God of vengeance; you require innocence in exchange for crime. It is the steam of blood which is pleasing to the jealous God! I owe him a victim, oh my daughter! and you are the victim!" [44] The daughter accepts, demands her two months' stay, departs with her companions to bewail her virginity, and returns "to offer herself to the paternal knife. This is what was sung by the daughters of Israel." [45]

Neither Vigny nor the author of Judges offers the slightest indication of the crime for which the hero and his daughter are punished. Jephté's vow may have been a rash one, and he is presumably guilty of original sin, and that seems to be all. In any case, he is grievously hurt, and his subsequent inclusion in St. Paul's splendid catalogue of the faithful (Heb. 11) hardly seems an adequate justification to reasonable eyes (Vigny makes no mention of it). One wonders why Vigny should have chosen him as a subject.

One answer is that, like Job, Jesus, Socrates, Tasso, and many another innocent victim of spectacular and unexplained misfortune, Jephté exemplifies a type of hero very fashionable in the Romantic period. Another answer is that Vigny already, at the outset of his literary career, is very skeptical of the goodness and the justice of God, and sympathetic to subjects which confirm his skepticism. As a result, he is now coming upon the kind of "humanism" which, growing steadily more solid and better defined over the next fifteen years or so, will constitute the unvarying basic idea in his masterpieces, *Chatterton, Servitude et grandeur militaires,* and *Les Destinées.* Like that of Samson in the latter collection, Jephté's real crime is his failure to have confidence in his own humanity, his needless purchase of divine aid by pledging sacrifices. He fails to realize that his strength lies not in the observance of taboos, but in himself. Thus he sins against humanity, and does so in the name and in the fear of Jehovah. And we are left with the impression that this God is mysteriously vengeful, ferociously capricious, inexplicably ruthless.

Vigny never published this poem separately. It has always appeared in collections, closely followed by *La Femme adultère.* It is possible that this pairing of the savage Jehovah and the merciful Jesus is intended to provide successive representations of the Old and the New Covenants. In the latter poem the Scribe is quite properly made to ask Jesus how the case is to be disposed of in accordance with the law of Moses, thus emphasizing the change from the old dispensation to the new. In any case, the Jehovah of both poems is a most unsympathetic figure; and the Jesus of *La Femme adultère* is much more man than god, and is faced, moreover, with a strikingly unrepentant penitent.

The image of God is not improved in *La Prison.* This work, dated 1821 by Vigny, presents the Man in the Iron Mask on his deathbed, in the presence of the priest brought in to shrive him. The text comprises 296 lines. The first twenty-nine lines show us the priest, a simple-minded and timorous cleric, being conducted blindfolded through a labyrinthine prison to the quarters of the dying man; he does not know whom he has come to serve. Having arrived, he hears the following exchange: "Prince, the holy man has come." "What difference does that make to me?" [46] Still without seeing his patient, the holy man begins his task of comforting and exhortation: your sufferings here have paved your way to heaven; as a priest I bring you your freedom; "the divine tribunal is sitting in this place. Answer. Already pardon is extended to you. God himself . . ."—and the dying man interrupts: "There is a God? Yet I have suffered much." [47] But the priest has his rejoinder: God has suffered more than you, shedding his blood for us ungrateful men; "bid, in his name, a manly farewell to life." "I was perhaps a King," says the dying man. "The savior was God," replies the priest, adding that priests too suffer much; he himself, for example, to forestall hell, wears an iron corset (sic) which makes even walking a torment, and for forty years his knees have been wearing down a flagstone in his cloister; "and even so much suffering as this is too little to purchase the ineffable hope of Heaven. One must be purified in the crucible of pain in order to conquer his place in the sacred abode"; wherefore hasten to make your confession, obtain absolution, and fall on your knees with me before the cross "on which God was lifted up for us." [48] So saying, he falls to his own knees beside the bed to offer the crucifix, and sees the prisoner for the first time. "Here is not a brow discolored by approaching death, nor the last ravages of the death agony; what he sees is without features, without life, without age: a motionless phantom reveals itself, and the torchlights gleam upon a mask of iron." [49]

The priest is horrified. The prisoner's plight is bad enough, but his own is even worse. Rumors pertaining to the Mask have run for many years, and he knows them; he knows especially that it is said that those persons who have had some contact with the Mask have shortly thereafter mysteriously disappeared. His role in the remainder of the poem is as it were electrified by his fear of a possible punishment which will not this time be self-inflicted. He nonetheless does his best to carry on with the task that he has come to perform.

But the Mask will not cooperate. He does not find the iron corset and the daily prayers impressive; not for him the "frivolous counsels" of this holy man. "Take a good look at me and then say that a God defends the cause of the innocent. Of all the proscribed sins, committed by all, not one has come between my cradle and my tomb. Alone, always alone, overcome by age and suffering, I die full of years, and have not lived." [50] He goes on to describe his imprisoned life and ends by weeping. The priest renews his exhortation, but now enlivened by his fear; one suspects that he is speaking as much for himself as for his patient:

"O my son, your life has run its course. Happy, thrice happy, the man whom God disciplines! Let us not spurn the pains which he inflicts: now is the time when your sufferings will be precious to you; he himself has prepared you for heaven. Forget your body, think only of your soul. God himself has said it: Man born of woman lives only a little time, and lives in sorrows . . . Here am I, like you, at the end of this life . . . It is my part to envy your long suffering which gives you the hope of a fairer world. The angels will open the holy place to you. Provided that you speak one word to your God, he will be satisfied." Thus . . . the old priest besought the dying man to pray, but in vain. [51]

Instead of praying, the Mask finds a moment of freedom in delirium, in which he recalls a momentary escape of years before; on the sunny shore of Provence he has been free and unmasked for a brief time, but the young girls have fled before him—all but one, who awaited him, unterrified by his identity: "I saw pity on her fair lips, and the gentle sparkling [*douces étincelles*] of her eyes in tears." [52] But he has been immediately retaken, and his freedom is ended. So too is his delirium; returning to himself, he sees the priest, who is weeping; "Ah! unhappy man, is it for your liberty?"

THE PRIEST
No, my son, I am weeping over you; eternity is at hand.
THE DYING MAN
For me! I don't want it; I should find chains there.
THE PRIEST
No, you will find only immediate favors. One word of repentance, one word of your faith, the Lord pardons you.
THE DYING MAN
O priest! leave me alone!
THE PRIEST
Say: I believe in God. Death is taken away from you.

[63]

THE DYING MAN
Leave my death in peace; my life was left there.—And with a last
effort the delirious slave breaks his dying arm against the prison
wall.[53]

And he dies unshriven.

The priest remains throughout the night, reciting prayers and
psalms, interrupted from time to time by his tears. On these
occasions he sprinkles holy water "on him who was perhaps
banished from Heaven"; then he resumes his recitations, a performance which is given piquancy by the probability that the
priest is thinking as much of his own plight as of that of the
dead man. The tissue of quotations, versified but otherwise
unaltered, woven here by Vigny is an interesting example of his
habit of adapting Biblical materials to serve a quite secular
purpose:[54]

O Lord! do not break my soul with your wrath; (a) do not involve
me in the death of the impious one (b) . . . When the evil-doer
spies upon me, (c) Lord, will you make me fall into his hands? It
is he who has broken your paths under my feet; (d) do not punish
me, for my crime is his crime. (e) I have cried to Heaven from the
deepest abyss. (f) Oh my God! bring me out from among the
evildoers! (g)

One is tempted to speculate that for the first time the priest
has found vital meaning in the Scriptures. We are told nothing
of his fate; the poem ends with his approach to look upon the
dead man's face, only to find the iron mask still in place
beneath the shroud.

The priest's god is one of cant, and his religion is a matter
of observing prescribed rules and gestures, complicated as much
as they are supplemented by the intrusion of real pity and real
fear. The Mask's god either does not exist or, if he does, he is
guilty of great injustice and cruelty. The Mask's doubt arises
from his unexplained sufferings, and in this he is very like many
other figures in Vigny's writings, not to mention Vigny himself.
The poet seems to have thought that a proper god should necessarily accede in his conduct to human notions of justice, thereby
procuring the happiness of those humans intelligent enough to
have these notions. Since God does not do this, Vigny puts the
idea of him further and further away as time goes on, and ends
by ignoring (or affecting to ignore) him completely. For us,

the interesting consequence of this attitude is the concomitantly increasing intensity with which Vigny scrutinizes man, coming in his maturity to place man's highest achievement in the works of the unaided and defiant human spirit which triumph over time. He will become, in other words, a humanist in the philosophical or theological sense, and of the purest kind.

Philosopher or theologian he was not, nor did he claim to be either (let us not be deceived by his so often repeated qualification of his poems as *philosophiques;* he visualizes himself as *penseur* ("thinker")—a thing different from "philosopher"). From the point of view of either of these disciplines, Vigny's conception of divinity, Christian or other, is pitifully poverty-struck. The fact remains that it is out of this conception that his humanism grew, and further that the work which makes him eminent among writers grew from this humanism.

The early (and decisive) expression of his view of divinity and its relationships to man occurs most fully in three poems, *Eloa, Le Déluge*, and *Moïse,* all of them of the first magnitude in the constellation of his works.

Eloa, ou la soeur des anges ("The Sister of the Angels") is his earliest triumph. Billed (after Byron) as a *mystère,* it is a poem in three cantos and 778 lines on the theme, so popular in its time (1823), of the redemption of Satan. Eloa is a very visibly female angel (Vigny will cite this ascription of sex to an angel as an example of poetic invention) who is born on Earth of one of the tears shed by Jesus over the death of Lazarus. She goes to Heaven, where she becomes very popular with her fellow angels, who admire her sweetness and beauty. There she hears of the parlous plight of Lucifer, begins to brood, resolves to save him, and departs on this mission. This is the content of the first canto, entitled "Birth." The rest of her story is quickest told in the titles of the remaining cantos: "Seduction" and "Fall."

This is by no means the most original or the most skillfully wrought of Vigny's poems, but it is surely the prettiest. Heaven sparkles and shines nicely in many colors. Golden harps, golden wings, white robes, brilliant sun, moon, and stars, appropriate jewels, appurtenances, customs, styles of speaking, and so on make up a satisfying picture very competently set in Alexandrine verse. Vigny makes liberal use of Milton, Byron, and especially Moore (*The Loves of the Angels*), to be sure; but the

French is his, and it is pleasant to read. The same is true of his Earth (Moore and Milton again, and also Chateaubriand); and all of these, together with Ossian and Monk Lewis, help out in Hell.

Despite his own abilities, however, and the skill of his models, Vigny has his troubles in this poem. A prominent one is a recurrent tendency to forget that he is dealing with the supernatural, and this embarrasses him a good deal. For example, introducing the important situation in Heaven in which Eloa learns of the existence and the fall of Lucifer, he begins his tale with the most natural expression imaginable: "one day"; and then, of course, he must immediately explain himself:

One day . . . (how dare one call by the name of day that which has no duration and no recurrence? Mocking the poverty of human language, Eternity veils itself from our intelligence, and in order to make us understand one of its short instants, it is necessary to find for them a name in the realm of Time).[55]

Milton gets into, and out of, the same scrape, and Vigny would have done well to imitate his incomparably smoother apology more closely than he did.[56] He would have done even better, I think, to dispense with "one day." But he did not; and so on this day Eloa receives from her rather bourgeois companions the information that it is possible for an angel to fall, and that one angel has in fact done so.

the fairest of us all is no longer here: nevertheless, in his pristine virtue he was called the *light-bearer*; for he carried love and life everywhere; he carried all the orders of God to the stars; the Earth consecrated his peerless beauty by giving the name of *Lucifer* to the morning star, that radiant diamond which the Sun placed amid his golden hair upon his rosy brow. But we hear that now he has no crown, that he groans, that he is alone, that nobody loves him, that the blackness of a crime weighs down his eyes, that he can no longer speak the language of Heaven; Death is in the words of his mouth; he burns what he sees, he withers what he touches; he can no longer feel either good or evil; he takes no joy even in the wrongs he has done. The Heaven where he lived is disturbed by the remembrance of him, no Angel will dare tell you his story, no Saint would dare speak his name.[57]

Eloa's reaction to this is not the execration expected by her colleagues, but rather a tear of pity. "She learned to ponder, and her innocent brow blushed, and it bowed, with this unknown perturbation." [58] Her reverie and her trouble produce her mission, and after a suitably described journey, she comes upon Satan; he appears to be a young man languidly lying upon a bed of vapors in the midst of a Chaos which at first sight seems to her to be "another Heaven." [59] The young man is wearing an irridescent red robe; he has black hair and wears a golden crown; his pale wings are folded; he wears golden anklets and diamonds on his feet; "his arms and all his fingers [*sic*] dazzle the eyes," and so on—the description is not felicitous. Equally routine, but faintly more interesting, is his "unquiet brow"; still routine, but decidedly more interesting, his eyes, which he keeps lowered, have in them "the involuntary flame which in a single glance reveals soul to soul." [60]

After an anodyne opening speech, which Eloa finds both frightening and charming, Satan embarks upon a self-description which occupies the bulk of the canto.

I am he who is loved and who is not known. I have founded my empire of flame upon man, in the desires of the heart, in the dreams of the soul, in the bonds of the body, mysterious charms, in the treasures of the blood, in the glances of the eyes. It is I who make the wife to speak in her dreams; the happy girl learns happy lies; I give them nights which console them for their days; I am the secret king of secret loves. [61] I have taken his feeble creature away from the Creator; despite him, we have divided Nature between us. I let him . . . hide golden stars under the brilliance of a Sun; for my part, I have the silent shadow, and I give to Earth the sensual pleasure of evening and the good things of mystery. [62]

And the monologue of this patron of sensuality continues for many more lines, including a pleasantly graphic, but still banal, account of an assignation. And then the speech concludes:

There you have the work of the Malefactor. This so-called evil one is a Comforter who weeps over the slave and steals from his master, saves him from the sorrows of his condition by love, and, buried himself in the evil common to all, gives him a little delight, and sometimes forgetfulness. [63]

Hearing which, Eloa, "struggling three times against an impure glance, veiled her azure eyes with a golden eyelid [*sic*]." [64] So concludes the second canto.

The opening of the third canto proceeds immediately with an apostrophe by the poet to the quality indicated by the veiling of Eloa's eyes: "Whence come you, Modesty, noble fear, O Mystery," coeval with Earth, "Rose of Paradise"? Assisted no little by the fourth book of *Paradise Lost,* Vigny traces Modesty's birth to the "forbidden tree": "Your charm is equal to that of the virtues, but you are also the first step towards evil." Before the Fall, Eve went uncovered, but Modesty, like crime, demands a veil. In the face of Satan's seductive onslaught, Eloa becomes modest, and this presages her defeat: "Already she was falling, for she blushed." [65]

The attack continues. Satan, "veiled like a winter sun," has revisited Heaven, wherein he found nothing to make him regret his former departure; only Eloa, in this realm pervaded by fear (Heaven), seemed to him to promise happiness, that good sought by all creatures; and she seemed "the Queen awaited by my solitary throne"; her presence, finally, "revealed to me that I was capable of love." [66] He goes on to describe his search for her throughout the universe, especially on Earth, where best, it seems, she could carry out her function as protectress of the innocent.

But the search was fruitless; "alone I returned to my fair dwelling, I wept there, as I do here, I groaned, until the moment when the sound of your flight stirred me and made me tremble like a priest who senses that his God is about to speak." [67]

The effect of this is to produce a gratifying degree of confidence and sympathy in the wavering girl-angel; filled with pleasure, she unveils her face, smiles sweetly, and comes closer to her companion; her fair bosom heaves its first sigh. And she speaks, but still with some puzzlement:

Since you are fair, you are no doubt good; for as soon as a soul takes its way to Heaven, its goodness, like a holy garment, gives it eternal beauty as it enters there. But why do your words inspire fear in me? Why is there so much sorrow printed on your brow? How could you bring yourself to descend from the holy place? And how can you love me, if you do not love God?[68]

As she speaks, her wings and arms and bosom glow with a light whose source is in all angels' hearts; "so does a diamond gleam amid shadows." And Satan, struck with fear and remorse, tries to shelter his eyes from the light. Thus begins the crucial passage of the poem. Satan shows himself to us entire, and Eloa misses her opportunity to redeem him.

Seeing again his wrongs in the depths of his memory, the accursed Angel bent his dark head; penetrated with an infernal sorrow, he said to himself: "Sad love of sin! sombre desires of evil! Gigantic thoughts of pride, of knowledge! How did I come to know your senseless ardors? Cursed be the moment when I measured myself with God! Simplicity of the heart! to which I bade farewell, I tremble before you, but yet I worship you. Am I less criminal because I still love you? But you will not return into my blighted bosom! I have come so far from what I was! so great is the distance from me to myself that I no longer understand the speech of innocence; I suffer, and my spirit, beaten down by evil, is no longer able to rise up to so much virtue.

What has become of you, days of peace, celestial days? When I, the first of those modest Angels, went to pray on my knees before the ancient law, and had not ever any thought beyond faith? Eternity opened to me like a festival, and, with flowers in my hands, rays of light on my head, I smiled, I was . . . I might perhaps have loved!"

The Tempter himself was almost charmed. He had forgotten his machination and his victim, and for a moment his heart rested from crime. He was repeating under his breath, his head in his hand: "If only I could know the tears of humans!" [69]

One is reminded, no doubt for cause, of Milton's Satan, for a moment "stupidly good" in the contemplation of Eve's beautiful innocence.[70]

Ah! if only the Virgin [Eloa] could have heard him at this moment! If only the celestial hand that she would have dared stretch out to him had grasped him repentant, willing to rise up again . . . Who knows? evil would perhaps have ceased to exist.[71]

But she does not hear him, and the gesture is not made. Instead, at sight of "Hell's convulsive grief" upon his brow, she is frightened and seeks to flee; Satan is thus brought back to his infernal self, and resumes his campaign of seduction, whose final and decisive strategy consists of his shedding tears. "The Virgin had not seen any tears in Heaven, and she stops," returns beside him, and weeps. What has she done to grieve him?—Sought to flee.—She would like to stay, but the Lord is waiting for her; she will intercede, and perhaps be listened to.—This will do no good; his destiny is fixed, and besides, Eloa is the only God who can save an Angel.

"What can I do? alas! tell me, must I stay?" "Yes, come down to me, for I cannot rise up." "But what gift do you want?" "The fairest gift is ourselves. Come." "Exile myself from Heaven?" "What does that matter, if you love me? Touch my hand. Soon we shall regard good and evil alike with equal scorn. You have never understood the enchantment to be found in offering your bosom to receive tears. Come, there is a happiness which I alone shall teach you; you will open your soul to me, and I shall fill it with that happiness . . . As a double torch joins its two flames, no less closely we shall unite our souls."[72]

For Eloa, the embodiment of pity, this argument is decisive. "I love you and I am coming down. But what will Heaven say?" Her question is accidentally answered by the words of a chorus of Angels which happens to be passing in the distance: "Glory in the Universe, in the realm of Time, to him who forever sacrifices himself for the salvation of another." "Heaven seemed to be speaking," says Vigny. "It was too much for her." [73]

Despite the sacrifice, the promised happiness does not seem to be forthcoming. Eloa wants to know why her companion is still so sad; "I thought I had saved you." On the contrary, says Satan, I am taking you away. She replies: "If we are together, it matters little where. Just keep on calling me your Sister or your God." The response to this is rather disturbing: "I am carrying off my slave; my victim is in my hands." And now he tells her that she has committed a crime. But she finds still one possibility of a kind of happiness: "Will you be happier, at least; are you content?" "Sadder than ever." "Who are you, then?" "Satan." [74] So ends the poem.

Thus the Pity engendered of the God-Man Jesus is doomed to waste itself eternally in the fruitless endeavor to bring happiness to the demon prince (or principle) of pride, sensuality, and knowledge. Eloa's determination to do this arises no doubt from the candid innocence of her character; it is also immeasurably influenced at precisely the proper moment by the message

of the fortuitously passing angel chorus. It is hardly surprising
that our stimulated and unsophisticated heroine should fail to
notice in the chanted beatitude the somewhat abstruse, but fatal,
limitation which disqualifies her. The glory in question is
awarded in the Universe (Nature) and in Time; it thus belongs
to mortals, not to angels. It is still a fact that she hears it at just
the moment when she is ripe for disaster, and that it confirms
her disastrous choice. To the extent that accidents are presided
over by divinity, it may be said that God dooms Eloa to an
eternity as the bride and slave of Satan as surely as he dooms
Jephté to the ritual murder of his own daughter.

We have seen that Vigny in *Eloa* tends to forget that he is
writing in the realm of the supernatural. By giving a sex to his
angel-heroine, by insisting so positively upon her femininity, he
makes her much more human than angelic. Anywhere at all,
she says to Satan, as long as it is with you; "just keep on calling
me your Sister or your God." Being then roughly undeceived,
she can still hope that at least she is making him happier than
he was. The knowledge that this hope too must eternally be vain
may be her final punishment—we are not told. In any case, this
most human of angels, compounded of pity and pride, whose
native country is, as Satan says, "a little closer to me" [75] than
that of the other angels, by her own will and choice abandons
Heaven, its splendors, its spectacles, its bliss, finding nothing
therein responsive to the needs of her soul softened by the
tale of Lucifer's exclusion; nothing in Heaven can remove from
her the "dream of an unfortunate Angel imploring her from
afar"; [76] and so at a given moment she spreads her wings and
sets out in search of him. She is driven by an irresistible desire
to soothe a sorrow which is none the less real for having a distant
and unknown victim. At the end of her search she finds the
Angel in whom the sorrow which she has come to soothe consists
precisely in his gnawing nostalgia for the Heaven which she
has left, a nostalgia quickened in him by her very presence. The
irony, for being obvious, is nonetheless present.

There is no direct reference in this poem to the presence or
the action of God. The reader is left to infer them. It seems clear
that Vigny, despite his supernatural machinery, is using his Eloa
and his Satan to represent the lot of the elite of humankind.
Like Milton, he seems to be declaring God's ways to man, but

he certainly makes no attempt to justify them. The theology of this poem is vague and barely visible. What is constantly and insistently before the reader's eyes is a very prettily decorated presentation of an already hackneyed figure, the Romantic poet-prophet, with particular emphasis upon the inexplicable but fatal frustration of this figure's desire to obtain beatitude for himself and for others. For no apparent reason, the desire and the talents necessary to realize it are sinful.

The nature of *Eloa's* God is confirmed and more elaborately expressed in *Le Déluge* of 1823. To a considerable degree this poem imitates Byron's *Heaven and Earth;* the general notions of Noah's Flood, rebellion, sympathy for the rebel, and an unreasonable and tyrannical Jehovah are all here. Here too is a very large quantity of imitations of details. Beyond this, the resemblances, proximate and numerous as they are, do not go. The poem's essential ideas and conduct belong to Vigny, and so does its rebellion.

For the Japhet of *Heaven and Earth* does not rebel. From first to last he is a man of faith, indeed of humble faith. His other most striking characteristic, I think, is his explicit, obviously sincere, generous and sympathetic love for his fellow men. He is hurt and puzzled to find that God does not appear to share this feeling; yet, while he has every reason to be outraged, he gives no sign of outrage, but rather acknowledges his incompetence to judge.

At the same time, there is some rebellion in Byron's poem; his angel characters, despite an ineluctable and incomprehensible divine will, are so attracted by the splendor of human love that they knowingly risk an eternity in hell in order to share it. Given this love, the human lot, with all its weaknesses and uncertainties, its sin and its mortality, to them seems preferable to an eternal, passionless ministry in God's presence.

Vigny's poem comes to much the same conclusion, but its conduct is substantially different. Like Byron, he calls *Le Déluge* a *mystère,* and he footnotes (to line 34) the identical verse quoted by Byron in his subtitle.[77] Like Byron too, he uses an epigraph; Byron's comes from Coleridge ("And woman wailing for her demon lover"); Vigny's is a translation of Gen. 18:23: "Wilt thou also destroy the righteous with the wicked?" [78] *Le Déluge* is much shorter than *Heaven and Earth,* containing

332 lines as against nearly 1200. It is written throughout in Alexandrine couplets. Some 200 lines are given over to description, mostly of landscapes; the remainder are narrative.

Only two characters appear prominently: Emmanuel, the off-spring of a union between an angel and a woman; Sara, a mortal loved by Emmanuel. These two are presented to us on the summit of Mount Ararat, where they remain throughout the poem, from the moment of dawn at which we first see them, to the shining of the rainbow as the water finally covers them.[79] Through what they say, we learn of other figures. Sara tells us that Japhet has introduced himself to her with a proposal of marriage, offering as bait the promise that, thus having joined the family of Noah, she will be saved from the coming destruction. She has left him without answering. From Emmanuel we learn of his angel-father, also named Emmanuel, who has fallen from grace because he loved a woman, and has departed to intercede with God to obtain pardon for his son (whose mother died in bearing him, and whose sin has consisted, apparently, in being the son of a sinning father). His words also imply certain things about the character of God. God is "irritated" and has therefore decreed the Flood; by his will, man will be destroyed not by war or disease or sorrow, but by an inanimate element; God visits the father's sins upon the children; God's justice is inscrutable: "The death of the Innocent is a mystery for man . . . The pity of mortals is not that of Heaven. God makes no treaty with the human race. He who created without love will bring death without hatred." [80] God's justice is mysterious; the innocent are punished with the guilty, but the family of Noah is not punished; God neither loves nor hates; God has no respect for human dignity. And the poet tells us that as soon as all earthly life (except of course what is in the Ark) has been destroyed, the rainbow shines, "all having been accomplished"— a conclusion not to be found in Genesis.[81]

Various anonymous characters are presented in the narration: an evil king and an evil pope accuse each other of having brought the flood upon the world; another king, "alone on his pyramid," despairs at the thought of the annihilation of his name and that of his race, whose mummies float past him as he thinks. The most interesting of the anonymities is "the last of the children of the chosen family [whom I cannot identify]" who, seeing the Ark pass by "like a wandering palace," wavers an instant and then shouts defiance. After this, he is "struck by lightning and reduced to dust."

This character is interesting because of his moment of hesitation followed by one of defiance, because of his satanic preference for the kingship of the dead over exile in a life in which he could not rule, and most of all, perhaps, because of his claim that the dead remains of his people will serve to astonish and humiliate the degraded generations to come. The thought underlying his speech is as unclear as his identity; apparently this person rejects a rescue, a salvation, to which he has some right, choosing to die with the rest of antediluvian humanity, whose doomed giants are "less guilty" than will be Noah's descendants, who will construct their new world upon humanity's tomb. Somehow he finds this prospect ignoble, and he finds the works of the giant bastard offspring of men and angels better and more lasting than those of the mere human beings to follow. Vague and fragmentary as the expression is, Vigny's notion here unmistakably foreshadows the belief that only that is dignified and beautiful which is made by human genius and human love despite divinity.

In *Le Déluge* it is Emmanuel who principally embodies genius and love. His name (a favorite with Vigny, who applies it to the hero of a number of his projects) means *God with us,* and this conception is carried out in Emmanuel's parentage and in his nature. Born to a woman who dies in giving him life, fathered by an angel who has knowingly abdicated his celestial status for love, loved by a woman who knowingly refuses her own salvation in order to remain with him, Emmanuel in his turn deliberately sacrifices for love his chance of achieving angelic immortality. Emmanuel senior, his father, departing to make intercession, has told him that he must come to the mountain alone: "Go alone to Mount Ararat, take its rocks as altars; pray, and alone, without thinking of the fate of mortals, keep always your eyes above the things of Earth.[82] . . . Be alone; if God hears me, I shall come."[83]

But Emmanuel's eyes continue to look upon the Earth, fixed there by the presence of the mortal Sara and his love for her. Their conversation, says Vigny, is "the last conversation of innocence and love."[84] Emmanuel has indeed returned upon the mountain to meet his father: "I have climbed Ararat"; but he has done so "with a woman." [85] For love, his forebears, angelic and human, have violated the purity of the divine order; now he is doing the same thing for the same reason, and with the same clear foreknowledge.

For Emmanuel has a gift of prophecy; and like many another prophet in and out of Vigny, he takes no pleasure in it.

> Oh! why have the veils of my eyes been removed? How have I come to know the secrets of the stars? Knowledge of the wilderness, annals of the shepherds! Last night, examining your divine heights of which Egypt and God only know the mystery, I was seeking in the Sky to know the future of Earth; my learned shepherd's crook, the pride of shepherds, was tracing the eternal order upon the shifting sands, comparing, in order to fix the hour at which the star passes, the pebbles of the plain to the gleams of space. [86]

This prophet is a shepherd. Vigny's first term for him is *pasteur*. [87] As such he possesses insights into the workings of the universe such as are peculiarly acquired by those who inhabit the wilderness and observe the heavens; and with his "learned shepherd's crook" he can write down the "eternal order." In so doing, he is functioning precisely as Vigny would have the poet function: by means of symbols, sometimes humble ones ("the pebbles of the plain"), he gives comprehensible expression to his glimpses of cosmic truths ("gleams of space", "the future of the Earth"). In so doing, he is trespassing upon knowledge which is the perquisite of God, thereby, we may suppose, compounding original sin. By means of his pastoral science he is able to predict the flood (one is reminded of Sophocles' *Oedipus the King*, whose hero, "untaught of birds," he says, is able to answer the Sphinx—he is likewise punished, in Sophocles, at least, for his sacrilegious claim to self-sufficiency).

With all his science, Emmanuel retains his reverence and remains faithful. Neither he nor Sara questions the divine judgment or rebels against destruction. Neither, on the other hand, shows signs of repentance, but only of resigned acceptance of a mystery. Knowing themselves condemned, without knowing why, embracing each other, they await the conclusion of their ordeal; painful it will be, but at least they will not be separated or alone: "Ah; let us praise the Eternal, he punishes, but he brings together!"[88] It is the work of "putting together" that these two find to be particularly divine.

I have already said that this poem is only about one-third narrative, and it is only to the narrative part that I have so far made reference. The descriptive part serves both as a pretty setting for the unfolding narrative, and as symbolic representation for the ideological situation in which the characters find themselves.

The poem's opening passage presents a nature still in the state of grace:

The Earth was still smiling and in its first flower; the daylight still had that same light that crowned the heights of beautified Heaven when God caused it to fall from his creating fingers. Nothing had altered the form of nature . . . Each treasure remained in its native element, without ever violating the celestial prohibition; and the world's beauty bore witness to its childhood; everything followed its own gentle law and its first inclination, everything was still pure.[89]

The only flaw is human: "But man was malicious."[90]

The most disturbing aspect of the coming cataclysm is that it will disrupt the divine first order of nature; henceforth, nothing in nature will be clearly in its place; on the contrary, man's effort to reconstitute the first order from the new one will haunt him with its fascination, and it will also constantly be frustrated. For knowledge there will be substituted uncertainty, doubt; and from now on the noblest of men will be he who, imitating God, will seek to put together elements of the new order in such a way as to re-create patterns of the old—thus, in proportion to his success, dispelling or diminishing doubt. Vigny's use of description to back these notions is not particularly subtle, but it is competent and pretty. For example, let us notice the following portion of Emmanuel's first speech:

How beautiful is the Earth in its immense roundness! Do you see how it stretches out to where Heaven begins? Do you see how beautiful it is in all its colors? . . . One would say that the vast landscapes are today sending up their incense, displaying their beauty, in order to touch, if possible, the irritated Lord.[91]

Thus Earth in the last moments of its perfection. But Heaven follows immediately:

But the vapors of Heaven, like black phantoms, bring all these noises, these lugubrious symptoms which, promptly at the prescribed moment, were [fated] to announce to the ruined Universe its death throes. Come, while horror surrounds us on all sides, while a vast night slowly crowns us, come, O my beloved! and, closing your fair eyes which are frightened at sight of the disorder of the Heavens, rest your head in my arms, on my bosom.[92]

So does the disorder of the skies announce the imminent dis-ordering of all of nature, and so does this passage divide itself nicely between still-persisting perfection and the foretaste of perfection's disintegration. A part of the prophet's role is to shelter and reassure humanity against the upsetting spectacle of change: "I shall tell you the moment when Heaven smiles, and during the danger my voice will speak to you." [93]

The character of the rest of the descriptive portion of *Le Déluge* is sufficiently indicated, I think, by these samples; it is articulate, pleasantly written, unoriginal, no doubt, but also altogether pertinent to the ideological scheme which it exists to decorate. Given the ideas, the description contains no surprises.

Taken all in all, this poem may fairly be called a well-made mediocrity. We may pardonably find it far more interesting for its ideas than for its fabrication. Here again, one may say that its ideas are interesting not because they are clearly stated (they tend to be murky), but because they are discernibly there at all.

These ideas may be reduced in summary to the following: (1) Original sin, whereby man, having violated God's basic and arbitrary command against seeking "knowledge of good and evil," falls from the state of grace and loses the perfect knowl-edge, *la science infuse*, that he had unwittingly had therein, retaining of it only a vague memory and an overpowering desire to regain it. (2) The accompanying change in the order of nature from its divine perfection in the antediluvian epoch to its chaotic fragmentation in succeeding time. (3) The passionless calm of God, who also refrains from entering into negotiations with man-kind.[94] (4) The shepherd-prophet who stands between God and man despite them both, who *is* God and man despite them both, and who represents the sole agency by which man's abiding desire to regain his lost state of grace may be in part realized. (5) The coupling of the poet figure with a female representation of love, which last provides the passionate energy that drives the poet to fulfill his function. It seems fair to say that the rest of Vigny's work, to his life's end, will be almost exclusively an exploration and an elucidation of precisely this combination of ideas. *Le Déluge* is important for us because it is the earliest such manifestation in the Vigny canon.

Moïse is earlier (if we believe Vigny's date for it—1822), but it contains only a portion of the complex presented in *Le Déluge*. The most important absence from it is that of a woman or a female component or complement to the prophet. It is in any case one of the most admired poems in French, and it is surely the finest of Vigny's poems previous to *La Maison du Berger* (1844). As triumphant verbalization, it is no doubt the best of them all. The Alexandrine is, as it were by nature, a line of much dignity; in rhyming couplet it is the French heroic meter. Nowhere, I think, is its inherent majesty more perfectly realized than in *Moïse*.[95] Vigny's Moses seems a tremendous figure, both in what he says, and especially in how he says it.

Since prosody is by definition untranslatable, the "how" must here be ignored. The "what" is considerable, but by no means new. Vigny has taken the already familiar figure of the poet-prophet and made it memorable by virtue of a superbly skillful composition.

Vigny himself sums up the "what" for us. My Moses, he says, "is not the Moses of the Jews. This great name serves merely as a mask for a man of all centuries, and more modern than ancient: the man of genius, weary of his eternal widower's condition [*veuvage*], and despairing to see his loneliness becoming ever larger and more arid as he becomes ever greater. Tired of his greatness he begs for nothingness. This despair is neither Jewish nor Christian; it is perhaps criminal; but such as it is, it seemed to me to lack neither truth nor elevation." [96] Moses' despair arises from the fact of his separation from the rest of mankind. The separation is caused by the fact that he is a man of genius.

As a man of genius, he has knowledge beyond other men of the truth of God and of the universe. He has great power over man and nature. His power comes from knowledge. He gives expression to this knowledge in such a way as to enable his fellow men to grasp it. Once a shepherd, like Emmanuel, he has become the shepherd of his people, having brought them out of captivity to the threshold of the land promised to their forebears. Like Emmanuel, he has knowledge of divine mysteries; the difference is that Moses has acquired this knowledge by the will of God, has used it to lead his people, and has expressed it in the laws which will one day enable those who observe them to enter into the Promised Land—that is, to procure their salvation, to regain paradise, the state of grace. Man, when he fell, was banished to the world outside of Eden, and this world thus became a house of death, a tomb. The accomplishment of Moses, according to Judaeo-Christian tradition, was the making of the first of the two keys wherewith Man will ultimately regain entrance into the house of life. The law of Moses is thus prophetic of the end of death, the death brought upon us by original sin. And the end of death must be the most momentous of human accomplishments.

And having done all this, and many other things besides, Moses, in Vigny's poem, stands above his people on the mountain; he looks over the whole of the new land, which they cannot see; and he knows that he, having brought them here, he, without whom they could not have come this far, may not enter into it with them. And this is one of the ironies of the poem.

The other may seem less profound to us than it presumably did to Vigny. Moses, the greatest of men, having been made so not by his own choice, but by God's, is wearied literally to death by his exalted condition: "What did I do to you, that I should be your chosen one?" [97] Vigny's line is presumably based on Num. 11:11. "Wherefore hast thou afflicted thy servant? and wherefore have I not found favour in thy sight, that thou layest the burden of all this people upon me?" But the Moses of Numbers is making common cause with God; the children of Israel are misbehaving; their leader's "affliction" is evidently his feeling that he is unequal to the task of properly managing all of them all of the time. "I am not able to bear all this people alone, because it is too heavy for me. And if thou deal thus with me, kill me, I pray thee, out of hand, if I have found favour in thy sight; and let me not see my wretchedness" (Num. 11:14–15). Whereupon the Lord instructs Moses to appoint seventy elders of the people to share the burden with him. There is no hint of this kind of frustration or weakness, or of God's cooperation, in Vigny's poem.

On the contrary, Vigny's Moses is begging for the termination of his function as the chosen one, not because he feels unequal to the appointed task, but because he thinks that he has sufficiently performed it without deviation or weakness; in so doing he has moreover suffered alienation from his fellow men; at least he has had enough and is unwilling to continue. God has made him "powerful," to be sure, but he has not made him divine. As a man, Moses is cut off from God; as a prophet, he is cut off from man; thus he stands utterly alone; and he returns time after time (four times in all) to the same refrain: he lives, and has lived, and fears that he may have to go on living, "powerful and solitary; let me die."

Moses' address to God occupies sixty of the 116 lines of the poem. The speech is divided into four parts, of which the first three enumerate the prophet's great accomplishments. The fourth (ll. 91–106) sums up his complaint and repeats his plea for death. The complaint alleges his solitude again, but here, and finally, emphasizing the absence of love: love of man for his fellows; love between man and woman. "From the moment that your breath filled the shepherd, men have said to one another: He is foreign to us. . . . I have seen love extinguished and friendship dried up. . . . My brow is too heavy to rest on a bosom, my hand leaves fear upon the hand that it touches. . . . Thus, far from loving me, they all tremble, and when I open my arms, they fall at my feet." [98] Like Vigny's Iron Mask, his Moses suffers the greatest privation that can be visited upon a human being; and he and the Iron Mask are the only heroes in Vigny's work who are thus deprived.

And both are thus deprived by a mysterious, absolute, and seemingly malign authority. We see nothing directly of God in *Moïse*. His existence is declared, and his presence is indicated in a cloud at the summit of "sterile" Mount Nebo; the cloud includes lightnings, and it is dark and black; God is King of Kings, the jealous God, the all-powerful. Beyond this, we can only draw inferences from the effects upon persons attributed to his will. Moses, we have seen, is made powerful, lonely, weary, unhappy. His election having passed to Joshua, the latter proceeds toward the Promised Land "pensive and turning pale." Moses, despite his services, may not enter the Promised Land; Numbers and Deuteronomy explain this prohibition; Vigny does not, but merely states it. It appears that Moses' plea for death is finally heard: "Soon the summit of the mountain reappeared [out of the cloud] without Moses.—He was wept for." [99] "Il fut pleuré"—the translation provides nothing of the irony of the expression. The phrase is cold, formal, matter-of-fact; it is the last reference to Moses in the poem; it is set parenthetically, giving the effect of being an afterthought; it ignores the thirty-days' mourning stated in Deut. 34:8; it emphasizes, by its nonchalant formality, the absence of personal feelings of the people for their leader. By its very neutrality it confirms the lovelessness which has been at once the reward and the despair of the prophet. And this intolerable situation results, it seems, not from some divine law applicable to all men alike, but from God's specific choice of one man in the multitude to be filled with his spirit and to execute his will. The power of God is unquestioned; but his justice is inexplicable, and his love is imperceptible.

Inexplicability, imperceptibility—these henceforth will be the principal attributes of God for Vigny. They are extremely obvious in the last two items of the *Poèmes antiques et modernes*. These are *Paris* (1831) and *Les Amants de Montmorency* (1832). By way of coda to this chapter I should like to comment briefly upon them.

Les Amants de Montmorency is a rather touching versification (118 Alexandrines) of a *fait divers* (a news item) of 1829 relative to a suicide pact (murder and suicide, in fact) carried out in an inn at the Paris suburb of Montmorency by a young clerk and his mistress. Vigny's rendition gives them an idyllic weekend in the country; all is forgotten but their love, and apparently they prefer ending the idyl in death to returning to the reality of the city. The poem is very pretty and very banal. The principals leave behind them, of course, a piece of verse, written by both of them; it is not quoted, but only described, in Vigny's poem: "Mad lines, without rhyme or meter.—An unfinished phrase stood alone at the top; an unanswered question, an inexplicable enigma, a question about death." [100] Vigny pretends to quote a fascinated chambermaid, whose fidelity to the lovers' memory comes, he presumes, from the fact that they had remembered to tip her. Whereupon he concludes his poem: "And God—Such are the times: they didn't think of him."

By these naïve young people, in other words, the enigmas of

love and death are altogether disconnected from the thought of God. Possibly the lovers had been badly brought up. But Vigny's comment applies not only to them, but to the age (*le siècle*). The poem's intention, not to say its conduct, is unclear; it seems possible that the closing line is no more than an afterthought. The divorce, in any case, is explicitly made. And the notion which apparently underlies it, namely, the inadequacy of the existing traditional view of divinity for the needs of men in the solution of overwhelming problems, is also basic to the poem which Vigny calls *Paris*.

This poem is dated January 16, 1831. It comprises 258 Alexandrine lines. Its problem is the mystery of civilization's purpose and destiny; its elaboration enumerates some current theories; its solution is blackness and night; its most used and most striking image is that of a circle. It is a more or less standard literary gambit to offer a view of Paris (a generally circular city) from some elevated location.[101] For many French writers— as for many of the rest of us, who may perhaps know better, the city is the epitome of civilization.

So it is, emphatically, for our poet. Vigny's imagery in *Paris* is nonetheless undecided, not to say helter-skelter. The city is first a "black circle";[102] then a "Wheel; and it is God's hand which holds and gives motion to its invisible axle";[103] two lines later it is the "pivot of France." The poet continues: "When the living Wheel hesitates in its rotation, everything hesitates and is shaken [*s'étonne*], and recoils in its course. The frightened spokes say to the rim: Stop. The rim says it in its turn to the rims whose crests are embedded in its own and turn under its authority. One relays [the word] to the other; and the impassive king, Paris, the immortal axis, Paris, the axis of the world, draws its motion from its profound vigor, communicates it to all of them, impresses it upon all of them, forcibly, and, from them, it receives no motion."[104] This development is as clumsy in French as it is in English. Vigny goes on to make matters worse, shifting his metaphor in turn to springs, scales, levers, gears, finally returning to "Paris the eternal" which is now the "divine hub [*moyeu*]" which "would turn without the Wheel,"[105] and concluding that "it is indeed . . . a Wheel in fact. Vertigo is sometimes prophetic."[106] One is inclined to wonder whether Vigny was in fact aware of the dizziness of this portion of his poem. This reader, at least, is struck by the badness of the writing. As in the case of *Moïse*, sense and image, taken in detail, are inconsistent and inept, while the Alexandrines which express them are majestic and impeccable—and the over-all message is reasonably clear.

The message is that man's old gods have once again become inadequate to the needs of his current civilization, wherefore he has turned once again to the search for new gods, or, more properly, new forms, in which to express his compulsion to worship. It is in Paris that the search is being carried on most intensively; it is from Paris that the next god will come. The poem concludes as follows:

In the chaos of fate, I know of only two certainties, SUFFERING AND DEATH. All men and all cities are going to them. But ashes, I think, are never sterile. If one day you find the ashes of Paris in your path, weigh them, and take us in your hand, and, seeing in its [Paris'] place a bare countryside, say that the volcano has exploded! Think on the triple labor that I have revealed to you [that of Lammenais, B. Constant, Saint-Simon], and reflect that above those of whom I have spoken there were yet others better and purer, rarities among all those who adorned their time . . . men full of love, and of doubt, and of pity, who were wont to say of the things of life: *I don't know,* who sought neither power nor wealth, and who, in their devotion . . . drank a hateful chalice to the dregs. Then, Traveller, you will leave the place, you will cast these extinguished ashes to the winds, and, raising your solitary voice in the soundless desert, you will shout: *"For a long time the world will be covered with night."* [107]

And the night was indeed to be dark and long-lasting, it seems. Nor is a full, unmisted daylight ever to come in Vigny's poetry. There is a gap of some eleven years between the last poem of the *Poèmes antiques et modernes* (1832) and the first which was to enter into *Les Destinées* (*La Sauvage*, 1843). It would be inaccurate to claim that *La Sauvage* follows logically upon *Les Amants de Montmorency*. But it is accurate to say that the collection *Les Destinées* follows logically upon the path laid out in the *Poèmes antiques et modernes*.

CHAPTER 3

The Master

THE eleven-year gap contains very few published works, and no new ones at all in verse. In prose, there are only three worth mentioning: the inept so-called novel *Stello* (1832), the famous drama *Chatterton* (1835), and the superb *Servitude et grandeur militaires* (1833–35). Unpublished (until 1912) was *Daphné*, composed, or at least worked on, in the late 1830's; this is Vigny's philosophico-fictional rendition of Julian the Apostate. *Stello* and *Daphné* both are experiments; both, despite the publication of the former, are unfinished; both may be called abortive. They serve, along with the rest of Vigny's prose (excepting *Servitude*) to show that it is in verse that he is truly a master.[1]

The chronological lapse is no more than that. Between the first and the second collections of poems there is no inconsistency, no shift in attitude or point of view. There is, to be sure, inevitably a deepening of perception, an increase in variety and subtlety of conception and expression, a new certainty in the command of the verse medium.

In this period too, Vigny had undergone three shattering experiences following closely upon one another: the death, in 1837, of the mother to whom he had always been exceptionally devoted; the cataclysmic termination of his relationship with Marie Dorval, in 1838; and the annoying, protracted, and (in the event) fruitless negotiations occasioned by the death of his wealthy English father-in-law, later in 1838; these last activities our noble hero found to be sordid (out of prejudice), inconvenient (he had to go to England to pursue them), and necessary (he was not nearly so well off as he thought he ought to be). These three occurrences appear to have operated effectively to put, so to speak, flesh upon the bones of his ideas, and to bring out in him a skill at modeling and nuance not hitherto evident in his work. The first and third of them we may, I think, take as read. The second, the affair with Marie Dorval, demands attention.

I Chatterton

Vigny's liaison with Marie Dorval probably began in the course of 1831; it terminated in August, 1838. Marie was by no means the first, nor would she be the last, of the poet's mistresses. One naturally assumes that every member of the rather lengthy list of women in his life, including the dull and sickly Lydia Bunbury whom he married in 1825 and served (in his fashion) as a model husband until her death, some ten months before his own, affected in one way or another his experience of his own being, and therefore had something to do with his work. In most cases, these influences are, if not problematical, at least tedious to adduce in a study as summary as the present one. But the affair with Marie Dorval was spectacular in many respects; furthermore, it bore surely and directly upon at least three of his works, two of them extremely important ones.

We may easily guess at the nature of this affair from a characterization of its principals. In most ways, they were almost ideally opposed to each other. Vigny was, among his literary peers, proverbially the gentleman-Romantic. Ever mindful of his centuries-old lineage, impeccable nobleman and officer, reserved and unfailingly proper in dress, speech, and manners, superbly correct in all of his dealings, he was, or fancied himself to be, the haughty and unwavering servant of the loftiest ideals in thought, art, politics, and sociability—and he stuck out like a sore thumb in the company of the more or less bohemian crew who were, with him, the stars of Romantic art and literature. He was meticulous in practical affairs and was also extremely annoyed by having to participate in them. Ideologically a kind of savior of humanity, he notably lacked the common touch, taking refuge, even as a candidate for political office, in the coldest sort of disdainful propriety. He mistrusted and scorned the mass of mankind; physical needs and monetary requirements seemed sordid to him.

He spent his lifetime complaining about his poverty; but, if he was never affluent, neither was he ever needy. There is not the slightest evidence that he ever, in the common meaning of the phrase, worked a day in his life. His money worries were plentiful, no doubt, but they had to do with inheritance and income. He was especially annoyed at not having sufficient income to maintain the domestic establishment and the social career that he thought fitting to his heritage, rank, and intellectual eminence. At no time was he poor; at no time had he to worry seriously over household bills or indebtedness. Lacking children (at least acknowledged ones), he was not concerned for their education or establishment. He spent his life moderately well off, able to afford not only the normal obligations of a householding gentleman, but also such other gentlemanly amenities as the maintenance of a bachelor flat suitable for the discreet entertainment of his series of mistresses, together with the customary gifts and other gallantries implied by such entertainment.

Marie Dorval's case is very different from his. The bastard daughter of a pair of obscure actors, she originated in the dregs of society. As a child of seven she began her stage career; when she died, aged fifty-two, in 1850, she was still a working actress. Twice married, she bore three children, at least one of them illegitimate. She belonged to a profession whose history in France is paradoxical: for centuries one of the most adulated there, for the same centuries it has been traditionally among the most denigrated.

Vigny, that is, was a very legitimate and reasonably comfortable somebody. Marie Dorval was precisely nobody. Not even her name was her own. As a child she wore her mother's name (Bourdais); as a teen-ager she married one Allan (*sic*), an actor who (possibly in memory of Diderot) gave himself the stage name of Dorval. Through one more marriage and a series of lovers, she was Marie Dorval.

It was in the theater that she passed her lifetime, and the bulk of that in the hardest, most ungrateful aspect of the profession: touring the provinces. After innumerable difficulties, she became a member (*sociétaire*) of the Théâtre Français; for various reasons, including her own obstinacy in matters of money, privileges, and prestige, her tenure there was intermittent and short-lived. Her obstinacy was partly temperamental; mostly, however, it came from an overwhelming and uninterrupted need for money. Money to maintain a queenly station and to pay the debts incurred for this reason, to be sure; but money above all to provide for and protect three extremely difficult children whose proper upbringing, a matter which she took very seriously, was fatally impeded by her frequent, protracted absences from Paris occasioned by the same need for money. It appears that Marie Dorval never knew a moment when the wolf was not noisily scratching at the door; it is also evident that she looked upon her responsibilities with an uneasy conscience and did her desperate and conscientious best to meet them. And she sought to meet them by means of her profession. Among her husbands and lovers, it is not recorded that any of them was better fixed than the relatively penurious Vigny.

From her letters to Vigny there emerge two prominent traits: her almost incredible devotion to conscientious hard work; an extraordinarily outgoing, garrulous, unreflective, and naïvely egotistical affection which, not incidentally, called most insistently for reciprocation and was fearfully pained when it was not immediately and amply supplied. Perennially preoccupied with the realities of a rather tawdry day-to-day existence in her profession, and above all with money and her concern for her children, Marie's letters must have seemed unutterably vulgar to the very pernickety and vastly more egotistical Vigny. Worse even than that, some of them caused him downright undignified inconvenience; not infrequently she asks him to check up on her children and her husband, deliver them messages, inquire into the disposition of the money that she has sent them, and report promptly back to her. To Vigny of all people such demands were distasteful, though on occasion he sought to meet them, only to be scolded, when he had reported, for being dilatory or inept. The scoldings were unquestionably deserved, but Vigny can scarcely have been pleased to be treated as major-domo or messenger-boy. Marie should surely have known better. But she obviously did not. And yet the liaison continued, at least without a definitive break, for some eight years.

The time-span is revealing. While neither party was "faithful" to the other over most of this period, neither party was conspicuously unfaithful. Each was justifiably convinced that the other was engaging in extracurricular activities in the interim.

Neither, I think, had base reasons (blackmail, profit, social advantage, or the like) to postpone or avoid a showdown. But the showdown was in fact avoided for a long time. Vigny's avoidance was apparently motivated by a combination of his care for his dignity with his genuine, if inexplicable, affection for a vital, talented, and basically honorable woman. It is more difficult to account for Marie's avoidance. Vigny had no wealth, nor did he ever pretend to her that he did have. He possessed relatively little influence, political, administrative, or personal, with the royal officers and functionaries who might conceivably have provided the security that Marie so badly needed. Considering simply the nature of the amatory relationship existing between them, she had ample reason to break with him even before her triumph in his *Chatterton* in 1835; afterwards, she had even more reason. But three more years elapsed, and the rupture, when it finally came, was made upon his initiative. One can only guess that they were for a long time, however illogically, in love with each other, and further that both of them knew this, and finally that both of them were aware of being illogical.

We are not particularly concerned with Marie Dorval's side of this relationship. For Vigny, it seems clear that most of what is meant by Woman in his work subsequent to 1831 was taught him by Marie Dorval; it is his relationship to her, more than any other of his experiences, which finally determined his conception of woman and of femaleness.

It was for Marie Dorval that he wrote the three plays which are his own: *La Maréchale d'Ancre* (1831), *Quitte pour la peur* (1833), and *Chatterton* (1835). The first of these undoubtedly visualized Marie as the versatile actress, above all as the theatrical darling of the emerging Romantic tradition, capable of interpreting the roles of the new movement far better than the reigning queens of the Théâtre Français, who shared that theater's conservatism and looked with suspicion upon the new plays. It was, after all, Marie Dorval who created certain of the most considerable roles in Romantic drama. In 1831 alone she was the first incarnation of two extremely important roles: the Adèle of Dumas' *Antony* and the name part of Hugo's *Marion de Lorme*; and, had she and Vigny had their way, she would also have created his *Maréchale d'Ancre*.

But it seems to have been with the person, rather than with the actress primarily in mind, that the lead roles of *Quitte pour la peur* and *Chatterton* were written. The former of these plays is vaguely witty and charming. Little of it matters here except one speech which, characterizing the heroine, seems tailor-made for Marie Dorval as Vigny must have seen her in 1833: "She has a soul which is candid in its aberration, frank in the midst of the falsehood of the world, tender in a cold, polished society, passionate in a time of apathy, pious in an age of irreligion" (scene 4). This view, while it is no doubt overfavorable and surely too neat, nevertheless seems to present Marie Dorval very much as she was in fact. The inexperienced and rather empty-headed duchess that she played in *Quitte pour la peur* is certainly not an idealized figure. Having taken a lover, the duchess discovers that she is pregnant by him, and is duly terrified by the prospect of her husband's vengeance. The duke, like most of the author's heroes an idealization of Vigny, informed of the situation, spends the night in a chair in his wife's room, talking pointedly of family honor and keeping her in fearful suspense as to his plans for vindicating it. At dawn he leaves, remarking that this unaccustomed visit to his wife's bedroom has effectively preserved appearances. He is very noble, very lordly, very knowing, very merciful, and rather disdainful in his protection of the errant wife, who is the victim much more of society than of her own vices.

There is no need whatever to look upon the events of this play as being biographical; but it does seem justifiable to see in the nature of its two principal characters and the relationship between them a sketch of Vigny's notions of Man and Woman as they should be in a highly sophisticated society. Woman is vain, passionate, pleasure-seeking, heedless of consequences, unable to bear unaided the social and moral responsibilities incurred by her activities. If she is weak, she is also charming, and her weakness is part of her charm. It is precisely this scatterbrained and lovely creature who serves to bring out in Man his greatest nobility and wisdom. Her very inferiorities, personal and social, inspire his courageous and knowledgeable efforts to protect her against the crushing inhumanity of social conventions.

These roles and relationships are basic also to *Chatterton*, where they are presented with much amplitude and complexity. This is Vigny's most satisfactory play; it is also one of the outstanding examples of French Romantic drama. In form and conduct it is an excellent realization of the bourgeois tragedy whose brilliant formulation some seventy-five years previously belongs to Diderot—a genre which, along with "serious comedy," its twin, seemed perfectly to satisfy the demands of *la philosophie*: that art must serve a morally useful purpose, and hence that the stage must be used as a pulpit. Such, indeed, was Vigny's explicit intention for *Chatterton*. The play's thesis—that the poet's function is to guide society and its institutions, and that society therefore owes the poet both respect and material support—was a favorite one of *la philosophie*. Vigny's own contemporaries declared for the first proposition, at least (notably Hugo, who incorporates it in *Hernani* and makes it the whole concern of *Ruy Blas*). And Lamartine gave moral support in the Chamber of Deputies to Vigny's effort to establish a decent copyright law.

Chatterton, which is set in London, has three principal characters: the eighteen-year-old poet Chatterton, an elderly Quaker who is also a medical man, and Kitty Bell, the wife of the rich and ruthless manufacturer in whose house Chatterton lives and dies in the course of the play. Among these three Vigny distributes the characteristics of the Poet as that figure will subsequently emerge in *La Maison du Berger*.

Chatterton is a young idealist who already has behind him a precocious poetic accomplishment: the *Rowley Poems*. He is very poor, very passionate, and very proud. Completely given over to his art, he is, as he says, quite useless for anything else. He has fallen in love with Kitty Bell, but has acknowledged this to no one but himself. He is dedicated above all to his mission as Poet. The play represents the critical moment at which he is shown with finality that the importance of this highest of all social functions is unrecognized by the humanity which he is called to serve, and that the function itself is looked upon by other men with amused contempt. The result is despair, the destruction of his manuscripts, and suicide.

The Quaker is one of several manifestations of a favorite Vigny character. Others are the Richelieu of *Cinq-Mars*, the Interpreter of *L'Alméh*, the Doctor Noir of *Stello* and *Daphné*,

the Libanius of *Daphné,* the Doctor Tronchin and the Duke of
Quitte pour la peur, the sea captain turned army major and the
Captain Renaud of *Servitude et grandeur militaires.* He is expe-
rienced, learned, disillusioned, and wise. He is calm, strong,
severe and detached, full of a condescending pity which he
conceals more or less badly, allowing it to burst into bloom at
moments of stress. The most complete example of this type is
the Doctor Noir. *Chatterton's* Quaker is distinguishable mostly
by being superficially Christianized. Like the others, he serves
as commentator, as a sort of all-knowing chorus, for the events
and relationships being displayed. As the Duke of *Quitte pour
la peur* is a sketched idealization of Vigny, so the sum, as it were,
of Chatterton plus Quaker may be called a fuller realization of
the same.

Kitty Bell may also be called an idealization of Marie Dorval.
Not Marie as she was, by any means, but Marie as Vigny might
have liked to remake her. A number of Kitty Bell's outstanding
traits, above all her capacity for generosity, affection, and maternal solicitude, were prominent also in Marie's makeup; at the
same time, Marie had others which Vigny deplored, and which
are either corrected or missing in Kitty Bell. We suggest, in
other words, that Kitty Bell is confected out of the "good"
traits of Marie.

Kitty Bell is above all a devoted woman. She is the very
dutiful wife of a man whom neither she nor anyone else can
love. John Bell's good qualities, probity, intelligence, industry,
and courage, are recognized by his friend the Quaker, without
whose references to them they might remain unnoticed. He is
also merciless, brutal, calculating, and servile; worst of all, of
course, he is altogether oblivious to any but material interests,
and altogether impatient of those who allege any others. By
this man Kitty is the mother of two young children whom she
loves with a passion which is more than maternal, being the
surrogate in part for the love which she cannot give to her
husband, and in part for the love which she has conceived for
Chatterton. With her extraordinary simplicity and discretion
Kitty combines an admirable piety and a charity so pronounced
as to induce in her a sort of hypocrisy quite alien to her nature
and to her sense of duty.

Her most prominent characteristics are exactly those which

were least noticeable in Marie Dorval: quietness, discretion, piety, and modesty. But the rest, just as exactly, belonged also to Marie Dorval: intense and devoted passion, impulsive simplicity, instinctive sympathy—despite ignorance and lack of understanding—for the immaterial concerns and the transcendental value of the Poet. It is unlikely that Marie Dorval could have been shocked literally to death, as Kitty is, by the death of the man that she loved; but it is not improbable that Vigny would have liked to imagine that she could be.

I suggest, in short, that for the character of Kitty Bell, that figure in his work which precedes and leads to the Eva of *Les Destinées*, in other words to the figure which embodies Vigny's highest and most eloquent idealization of Woman, the model was Marie Dorval.

No other heroine in French Romantic fiction, prose or verse, novel or drama, is characterized with more delicacy, subtlety, nuance, credibility, or sure-handedness than is Kitty Bell. And her peers are rare in the first fifty years of the nineteenth century: Stendhal's Mme de Rênal (*Le Rouge et le noir*) perhaps; perhaps also the Bette, the Mme de Mortsauf, the Mme de Beauséant of Balzac (*La Cousine Bette, Le Lys dans la vallée, Le Père Goriot* and *La Femme abandonnée* respectively); possibly the Camille of Musset's *On ne badine pas avec l'amour*. Certainly Kitty is unequalled elsewhere in Vigny's work. And there is no evidence that any other woman in Vigny's life (except possibly his mother) penetrated so deeply, so diversely, and so exasperatingly into his consciousness, into the fabric of his life, as did Marie Dorval.

Were this fact (if it is one) meaningful simply for *Chatterton*, it would scarcely be worth emphasizing. But the concept Woman becomes an all-important component of Vigny's ultimate metaphor for the Poet, and it is upon his work as the Poet's expositor and apologist that his survival depends.

Unlike *La Maison du Berger, Chatterton* does not visualize the Poet as an integration of male and female elements. Vigny had not yet, in 1835, come clearly upon such a formulation, although it is hinted at in certain earlier writings, e.g., *Le Déluge, Eloa, Héléna*. The effect of Kitty Bell upon Chatterton is indeed rather more to confuse him and distract him from his work than to aid him in carrying it out. The Quaker, who, so to say, sees all and knows all, looks upon the unspoken bond between them as implying some impediment to Chatterton's fulfillment of his calling. Speaking strictly in terms of the play's thesis, one is compelled to say that the role of Kitty Bell is largely unnecessary, if not altogether extraneous. She is touching, picturesque, endearing; she was also played by Marie Dorval. No doubt these qualities compensated for her substantial uselessness. It is certain, in any case, that it was her role, and not the play's thesis, which underlay *Chatterton's* very considerable success with the contemporary public. For us, however, its interest lies in its thesis.

The latter is most succinctly expressed in Act III, scene 6. Beckford, the Lord Mayor of London, has come to rescue Chatterton, the son of an old friend, from his appalling indigence. He asks him the following question:

A good Englishman must be useful to his country.—Let's see; what is your idea of the duties of each and every one of us?

CHATTERTON

I think I understand them, milord. England is a ship. Our island has such a form: her prow turned to the north, she is so to speak at anchor in the midst of the seas, overlooking the continent. She ceaselessly draws from her side other ships made in her image, which go to represent her on all the coasts of the world. But the work of all of us is aboard the great ship. The King, the Lords, the Commons are at the flagstaff, the wheel, and the compass; all the rest of us must handle the lines, climb the masts [sic], spread the sails, and load the guns; we all belong to the crew, and none of us is useless in the handling of our glorious vessel.

LORD BECKFORD

Not bad! not bad! though he's still making poetry. But, even admitting your idea, you see that I'm still right. What the devil can the Poet do in handling the ship?

CHATTERTON

He reads in the stars the path shown us by the finger of the Lord.

LORD TALBOT

What do you say, milord? do you call him wrong? The pilot is not useless.

LORD BECKFORD

Imagination, my dear fellow! or madness—it's all the same. You're good for nothing, and you've made yourself that way by such stupidities.

Chatterton's notion of the Poet's function is crystalline, and I trust that the nature of the Lord Mayor's role is sufficiently indicated by the excerpt.

Kitty Bell's share in the provocation of Chatterton's exalted views is unwitting and only vaguely positive. It appears that, although she may not have inspired them, she has at least provided a favorable climate for their germination. So the Quaker would lead us to believe. He says to her, in Act II, scene 5:

This young man whose mind has ripened too rapidly under the ardors of Poetry, as though in a burning hothouse, has kept the naïve heart of a child. He no longer has any family, and, without admitting it to himself, he is looking for one. He has become accustomed to seeing you near him, and perhaps he has acquired the habit of being inspired by the sight of you and of your maternal grace. The peace which prevails around you has been as dangerous for this dreaming spirit as slumber under the white narcissus.[2] It's not your fault if, rejected on all sides, he now considers himself blessed with a sincere welcome. In any case, this atmosphere of deep and quiet sympathy has become his own. Do you think that you have the right to take it away from him?

The Quaker here is answering Kitty's scrupulous alarm at having aroused Chatterton's affection by assuring her that because of her the Poet will be able to continue his proper work. Kitty's conventionally moralistic misgivings are countered with a plea for tolerance in the name of inspiration and dream. The Quaker evidently thinks that she may provide it. So far, and no farther, goes the function of Woman in the composition of the Poet as it is set forth in this play.

It is understandable and also a bit ironical that *Chatterton* should endure because of Kitty Bell. The splendor of her role is matched by the utter mediocrity of the remaining ones, numbering five, exclusive of walk-ons. This phenomenon is symptomatic of two things, at least: first, of the fact that the play was written for Marie, together with all that that implies; second, and perhaps more important historically, that while the war of literary forms had been finally won at the battle of *Hernani,* the war of poetic ideas was still being unclearly envisaged and unclearly fought, five years later, by Vigny.

Clarity will shortly be forthcoming, immeasurably stimulated by the closely succeeding agonies of the death of Mme de Vigny senior (December, 1837) and the break with Marie Dorval (August, 1838). These events obviously served to exacerbate Vigny's sensitivity to the notion of Woman and what she meant to Man (Vigny himself, as always). From his experience of these two women, it appears, Vigny came to formulate finally the idea of femaleness as an indispensable component of that hitherto very male species: the Poet. Mother and Marie at first served him well, the one as a model of loving and sympathetic understanding, the other as the charming but hypocritical and heedless negation of this quality, the thoughtless, materialistic, egotistical traitress. As the years went by and the wounds began to heal, Vigny tended to bring the two figures closer and closer to each other. He thus approached, but never achieved (nor, I am sure, did he seek to achieve) the miraculous fusion of the two which is Woman in Baudelaire's *Les Fleurs du mal*. But the indispensability of the female component of the Poet is extremely clear and abundantly expressed in the masterwork which is the collection *Les Destinées*.

The earliest published of these is *La Sauvage* (1843). But the earliest written, as far as we know, is the poem made in 1838 on the rebound from the painful parting from Marie Dorval. This is *La Colère de Samson*. And it is with this poem that I wish to begin our consideration of the posthumous collection.

II   Les Destinées

Vigny's claim to eminence in French poetry will probably continue to be based almost exclusively upon this group of eleven poems, published posthumously (1864) by his friend and literary executor Louis Ratisbonne. It was Vigny, not Ratisbonne, who had for years puzzled over the constitution of the collection, the choice of the poems to be included, the order in which they were to be presented. Ratisbonne was apparently a faithful executor; there seems to be no good reason to doubt that the choice of items and their order represent Vigny's own latest wishes. The poet's posterity, considered in more general terms (the literate public, anthologists, textbook writers), tends to give primary importance to seven of them: *Les Destinées, La Maison du Berger, La Colère de Samson, La Mort du loup, Le Mont des oliviers, La Bouteille à la mer,* and *L'Esprit pur.*

Seven items in the collection had been published separately previous to their grouping by Vigny-Ratisbonne, all of them in the *Revue des deux mondes*: *La Sauvage, La Mort du loup,* and *La Flûte* in 1843, *Le Mont des oliviers* (excepting its seven-line postscript) and *La Maison du Berger* in 1844, *La Bouteille à la mer* in 1854, and *La Colère de Samson,* as an advertisement for the collection, in 1864. Some of these poems, perhaps all of them, were topical or topically inspired: the obvious examples are *La Colère de Samson,* as mentioned above, *Les Oracles,* which embodies the poet's disillusionment with the Bourgeois Monarchy, the disquisition on the evils of railroads in *La Maison du Berger,* and *Wanda,* which has to do with the Russian autocracy's lamentable practice of transporting dissident but otherwise respectable nobles to slavery in Siberia. It is none-theless evident from the selection and the order of the poems as finally published that topicality and chronology of composi-tion were the least important considerations in the making of the book. It seems undeniable that in Vigny's mind this book was to be his final statement to civilized humanity, whose dis-tinguished, if unrecognized, servant he thought himself to be.

The preface to the collection *Les Destinées* is the poem *Les Destinées.* Like all good prefaces, it was written long after most of the other poems it was designed to introduce. We shall con-sider it in due course.

La Colère de Samson is something else. Unlike the other poems which accompany it in the collection, it was apparently sketched by a very wrought-up author, then somewhat revised, and eventually completed and put aside to await its writer's death. Most Vigny *aficionados* make a game out of the undeni-ably biographical aspects of the poem. Our present purpose commands that we ignore them. We are concerned purely and simply, according to its author's wish, with a *poème philos-ophique,* with a production which, whatever its origin, was deliberately included, after many years of mature and presum-ably dispassionate consideration, in the group meant to be its author's last testament.

Then what is *La Colère de Samson* for us? It is, I suggest, a negative statement of the nature, the needs, and the function of the Poet. Samson in this poem is very strong. His muscles are beyond compare. In addition to his muscular prowess, he has the very peculiar advantage of being a Nazarite; as long as his hair remains uncut, he believes, his muscles will remain peerless. According to this poem's plot, Samson has his hair cut; he is taken immediately to the Philistine temple; he thereupon pulls it down upon his own head and that of his enemies. It is evident that for Vigny the length of Samson's hair is quite irrelevant. The Nazarite notion, in other words, is simple nonsense.

Samson is a fool on two counts: (1) He has believed in the Nazarite thing and therefore failed to trust his muscles. (2) He has confided his secret to the Dalila who he knows will betray him. Samson, in short, is an ass. A part of his asininity resides, as he says, in his more or less mistaken dependence, sexual, moral, psychological, what will you, of male upon female. This dependence, in his view, (but possibly not in ours) is God's fault; I quote:

Man always needs caresses and love; his mother bestowed them on him from his first moments; it is her arm which first lulls and rocks him and gives him a desire for love and indolence. Disturbed in his activity, disturbed in his planning, everywhere he will dream of the warmth of the breast, of night songs, of kisses in the dawn, of the burning lips which his lips devour, of the unbound hair which inundates his brow, and as he proceeds, the nostalgia for the bed will follow him. . . . When the combat made by God for his creature, against his fellow-man, against Nature, forces Man to seek out a breast on which to lean, when his eyes are in tears, he must have a kiss.[3]

Vigny's Dalila, like the biblical one, turns out to be a bit of a stinker; his Samson screams to us for sympathy. Vigny's very non-Scriptural version of the end of Samson's story should be sufficient indication of the poet's view of the situation. Out of weakness, stupidity, subservience, Samson fails to recognize himself as being a self-sufficient entity. No gods, for Vigny, need apply. But for the soft and possibly deluded Samson, femaleness, Woman, he thinks, is essential. And since the Dalila, the particular woman of this poem, is no more than flesh, poor Samson is defeated. His defeat symbolizes the abasement of the well-equipped, talented man who hitches his wagon to a purely fleshly star. Samson's complaints are merely contemptible. In the scheme of *Les Destinées*, he is an antihero, an exception to prove the rule. The rule is illustrated in the other poems in the group. But first, the ideological context in which the rule exists is provided by the prefatory poem, also entitled *Les Destinées*.

This one has an epigraph ("It was written"); it comprises 123 lines written in a deliberately plodding *terza rima* (approximately) of Alexandrines. It has no hero, but rather a set of heroines, who are "les Destinées":

These cold deities bound the leaden yoke upon the skull and the eyes of Men, their slaves, all of them [men] wandering, without a [guiding] star in an infinite wilderness . . . Sad divinities of the Eastern world, women veiled in white, immovable statues, they crushed us under their colossal weight.[4]

The arrival of Jesus upon earth seems to change things:

One night, it happened that the ancient planet shook off its dust.— A great shout was heard: "The Savior has come. . . . His brow is bloody, and his side is wounded, but Fatality is dying at the feet of the Prophet; the Cross rises up and spreads over us like a shelter!" . . . Removing the heavy knots of the leaden yoke of Fate [this is Vigny, not his translator], all the Nations cried together: "O Lord! is it true? is Destiny dead?"[5]

Our heroines rise up to God and protest this apparent alienation of their authority. They are answered by a voice from on high:

Return in my name, Queens; I am Grace. Man will always be an uncertain swimmer in the waves of time which is measured and which passes. You will touch his brow, oh daughters of Destiny! . . . He will be happier, thinking himself [his own] master and free, struggling against you in an evil fight in which I alone, on high, will hold the scales.[6]

Thanks to the Savior's intervention, it appears that mankind has a very slightly less limited activity than previously:

Stronger now, in this somber duel, our soul in mourning fights against these impassive Spirits. Sometimes we raise up their false and cruel fingers. Our will carries up to sublime heights our brow illuminated by a ray from heaven.[7]

For all that, man's prospect is not joyous. It is puzzling,

mysterious; there may be room for hope, but one cannot be sure. The advent of the Christ has been shocking, but the meaning of his advent remains imponderable:

Unanswered question, about which your Saints have remained silent! O Mystery! O torture of the strong and serious soul! Is our eternal word: IT WAS WRITTEN? the enslaved Orient says: ON THE BOOK OF GOD; and the Occident replies: ON THE BOOK OF THE CHRIST.[8]

Man in his history, in other words, has witnessed in the coming of the Christ an apparently epoch-making event whose real consequences are still so indecisive as to be negligible, if not downright illusory. The writing in the book of the God of the Orient is answered in the West by the writing in the book of the Christ, to be sure; but this appears to be a distinction without any essential difference. The forms have changed; the substance remains mysterious; as nearly as one can guess, from this poem and its fellows, the substance remains unchanged. Man's relationship to God remains incomprehensible. Man is therefore (I speak now of the rest of the collection) forced to find his dignity without reference to divinity, solely in himself. Such is the burden of this collection. So it is most heart-rendingly expressed in *Le Mont des oliviers*.

Vigny presents us here with Jesus in the garden of Gethsemane. Like the Moses of his earlier poem, this Jesus is a figure for the Poet. He differs from the Moses in two essential aspects: he has undertaken the communication of truth to mankind without Moses' resentment; he is unable to obtain God's permission to complete his task and therefore refrains, griefstricken, from doing so.

Le Mont des oliviers contains 149 Alexandrine lines, divided into three unequal parts and a postscript. Part II, the longest (95 lines), is spoken by Jesus; it summarizes his accomplishments, notes that already they are being vitiated, and goes on to enumerate the even vaster ones which, with God's consent, he could perform. Having introduced the idea of brotherhood to man, and substituted spirit for flesh, symbol for substance, in his worship, observing that now these doctrines are being falsified and perverted,[9] Jesus begs to be allowed to remain alive until he has finally removed Evil and Doubt from the mind of man. "With one word I can reduce them to dust. . . . Let me absolve you from having permitted them. This is the accusation that weighs down upon the whole of creation." [10] The secrets of Nature, Earth's role in the universe, the relationships between truth and falsehood, justice and injustice, the existence and the prosperity of evil, the punishment of innocence, the death of children—for these and other problems of similar scope he can provide the solutions. But no answer is forthcoming from God, and Jesus resigns himself: "Your will, not mine, be done, and for eternity." [11]

The seven-line postscript has a title of its own: *"Silence."* It reads as follows:

If it is true that in the sacred Garden of the Scriptures the Son of Man said what is reported here; if Heaven, mute, blind, and deaf to the cry of creatures, left us like an aborted world, the just man will oppose disdain to absence, and will henceforth respond only with a cold silence to the eternal silence of Divinity. [12]

Parts I and III of this poem are descriptive. Surely this is the blackest poem in French. The postscript's message is well represented in Vigny's choice of illumination. There is a plethora of night, of shadow, of death: "night" (1. 1), "corpse" (1. 2), "sinister wind" (1. 4), "sad unto death, his eye gloomy and shadowy" (1. 6), "thief in the night" (1. 8), "black sky" (1. 13), "sleep of death" (1. 19), "a cloud in mourning is spread like a widow's veil" (1. 24), "seeks without seeing" (1. 137), "like mourning marble all the sky was black" (1. 138), "the earth without lights, without a star, without a dawn" (1. 139).

Against all this blackness, only two lights are set. Jesus is "dressed in white, like a corpse in its shroud" (1. 2), and the poem ends as he sees "the torch of Judas" (1. 142). Somehow the lights seem even more deadly than the blackness. Death is man's ultimate physical disgrace; treachery, for Vigny as for Dante, is the ultimate immorality.

Ignored by God, impersonally and ruthlessly crushed by Nature, unheeded (Vigny keeps the sleeping disciples [11. 18–20]) and betrayed by the men whom he has loved and taught, his message fragmentary, misunderstood, perverted—such is the destiny of this Jesus. His accomplishment, potentially so great, is an extremely limited one. He has brought a new word—Brotherhood—into human consciousness, and he has provided new and rich forms for man's worship. But that is all. He has not changed man's need to worship, nor has he changed either the object or the futility of worship. Despite the new forms, the old, fruitless activity goes on as always. Here, as in the poem *Les Destinées*, the fabled Christian liberation is merely an illusion worked by a change of name and of costume.

Thus it would seem that poetry and prophecy must be forever doomed to remain ineffectual pipe-dreams. And such is also the burden of *Les Oracles, La Colère de Samson,* and *La Mort du loup* in this collection. But such is not the whole message of the book.

The key to the whole is provided by *La Maison du Berger,* which, following immediately in order upon *Les Destinées,* is evidently intended to complement and correct the latter poem's declaration of the utter frustration of the human spirit. This splendid work is Vigny's masterpiece in verse; first, it epitomizes his notions of the Poet, his nature, his thought, and his art, and the relationships between these things and the rest of his physical and metaphysical circumstances; second, it does so in 336 well-wrought Alexandrines put together to form a beautifully eloquent and coherent poem.

La Maison du Berger is divided into three parts (133, 91, and 112 lines respectively). It is subtitled "Letter to Eva." Vigny scholars for a century have speculated about the identity of Eva. Under his pen she is not the "Eve" that a Frenchman might be expected to write. Most speculations are biographically directed, and most conclude, unsurprisingly, that the name may represent one or more of the several women who at one time or another shared Vigny's bed. Research on this point has been further titillated by the facts that *L'Esprit pur,* the concluding poem in *Les Destinées,* is also addressed "To Eva"; and the first stanza of *Les Oracles,* the poem which follows *La Maison du Berger,* is directed to a "Daughter of the Ocean," and makes it clear that this figure is identical with that of the addressee of *La Maison du Berger.* As long as it remains biographical, the "Eva" problem is properly relegated to footnotes. It is here placed in the text because its import seems much more ideological and symbolic than biographical. Nearly the whole of the third part of *La Maison du Berger* is given over to answering the question which introduces it: "Eva, who are you, anyway?" [13] For this reason, at least, biographical research, however fascinating, seems irrelevant.

Part I is equally divided between a recommendation that Eva join the narrator in a rustic and elevated solitude, thus withdrawing from citified mundanity, and a diatribe against the railroad. In tribute to Vigny, it should be emphasized that the latter is so cast as to seem not inappropriate in a predominantly metaphysical poem. Part II is an apostrophe to Poetry, accompanied by a commentary. Part III describes Eva, and also Vigny's view of man's relationship to physical and metaphysical nature. In form, the poem is a collection of seven-line stanzas, rhyming *ababccb* without linking rhymes between stanzas.[14] Its line is the majestic Alexandrine.

Given the importance of Eva in this and other poems in the collection, it seems advisable to begin our examination of *La Maison du Berger* with Vigny's description of her in Part III. Here it appears first that Eva is simply a name for Woman, a gift of God to Man, a gift, moreover, whose value and history are somewhat difficult to determine. "Do you know," says the narrator to Eva, "that, in order to punish man, his creature, for having touched the tree of knowledge, God permitted that man should, above all, in all times, at every moment of his life, find his sovereign good in self-love, [that he should be] tortured by loving himself, tortured by seeing himself?" And so God created Woman to be a doubtful, or at least ambiguous, alleviation to this situation: "But if God placed you beside [Man], oh woman, delicate companion, Eva, do you know why? It was that he might look upon himself in the mirror of another soul, that he might hear the song which comes only from you:—Pure enthusiasm in a sweet voice. It was that you might be his judge and his slave, that you might reign over his life while living under his law." [15]

Eva begins to be fascinating. Despite appearances, she is not at all Faust's "Ewig-weibliche" which "zieht uns hinan"; she is no savior in any sense, least of all in a Christian one. Taking Vigny at his word in these lines, we may say that she is created by God to mirror, to reflect, in at least one sense to redouble, man's besetting torment, which is his loving contemplation of himself. She is to sing her peculiar song: pure enthusiasm. Now, *enthusiasm* is not a casual word in French Romanticism. Madame de Staël's etymology, "God in us," had already (1810) popularized and somehow licensed the term as designating the divine spark, or fire, or inspiration, or "original genius," in short an essential quality of the Poet and of Poetry. "Your thought [Eva's]," Vigny goes on, "leaps like a gazelle."[16] "You have nothing of our [masculine] prudence, your heart vibrates and resonates with the cry of the oppressed. . . . Your fiery words move the masses, your tears wash away insults and ingratitude. You nudge man . . . he rises up in arms. It is you who hear the great plaints voicelessly exhaled by sad humanity." [17] But the essential, the indispensable raw material must be refined and disciplined in order to be useful; "your thought," we repeat, "leaps like a gazelle, but cannot walk without guidance and support. The ground bruises its feet, the air wearies its wings, its eye blinks in the light when the light shines; sometimes having soared in one bound to a high place, your unstable thought, disturbed by the sound of the winds, cannot stay there without fear or anxiety." [18] Feminine enthusiasm, in other words, needs to be coupled with masculine discipline in order to be effective. Each element, feminine and masculine, complements the other; it is only in the coupling of the two that humanity's significant work is done. Man's work, that is, is done solely in "sinful" self-contemplation. And here we may identify Vigny's view with that of Baudelaire.

The situation calls irresistibly for a sexual image, and this is provided in Part I, as we shall see. In the meantime, Part III continues with a dazzling juxtaposition of the work of the dual Poet with a characterization of Nature which, for its date, at least, is surprising. "Eva," says the narrator to her, "I shall love all created things, I shall contemplate them in your dreaming eyes which will cast everywhere their colored flames, their gracious tranquillity, their magic flavor: Come and place your pure hand upon my torn heart; never leave me alone with Nature, for I know her too well not to be afraid of her." [19]

"All created things": those things which have had a beginning, and hence will have an end. Mortal things, transitory things, things which are not eternal. The narrator will love these, and these not as he sees them with his own eyes, but rather as he sees them reflected—distorted, colored—in Eva's eyes.[20] Apparently his love, and presumably therefore his credence, goes rather to the reflection than to the thing reflected. It seems that, for him, only that is valid and valuable (I do not say true) which has somehow been subjected to the operation of a human organism. Against this notion, and in order to emphasize the point, Vigny places a twenty-one-line speech in the mouth of Nature,[21] a speech whose purport is expressed adequately, for our interest, in lines 288–89: "I rotate disdainfully, neither seeing nor hearing the peoples [of mankind] alongside the ants"; and (l. 292): "They call me a mother, and I am a tomb." And then comes the narrator to wind the whole thing up with a seven-line post-script[22] which he concludes by admonishing his eyes to "love that which never will be seen twice."

Four stanzas remain in the poem. The first and the third apostrophize Eva; the fourth brings Eva and the narrator together in a not unexpected conclusion: "Thus we shall walk, leaving only our shadow upon this ungrateful earth where the dead have passed; we shall talk together of them at the hour when all is dark, when you like to follow an obliterated road, [when you like] to dream, leaning against wavering branches, weeping, like Diana beside her fountains, for your silent and constantly threatened love." [23]

The second of these stanzas is the best known passage of the poem, and one of the best known in French poetry. It is the famous apostrophe to Nature which translates as follows: "Live, cold Nature, and relive unceasingly, under our feet, over our heads, since this is your law; live, and, if you are a goddess, disdain Man, the humble passenger, who was to have been king over you. More than all your realm and its vain splendors, I love the majesty of human sufferings. You will receive no cry of love from me." [24]

All of this had already been strikingly said, as Vigny well knew, by Pascal, who had made of man "a reed, the weakest thing in Nature, but a thinking reed"; and for both Pascal and Vigny, man's dignity resides in his capacity for thought. It must be added that while the meaning of Thought is not the same for Vigny as it is for Pascal, the two agree verbally, at least, that this possession is man's distinguishing characteristic. On Pascal's scale of values (derived, apparently, from St. Augustine), man is thereby exalted to a condition of mediocrity. Vigny, who is being snooty about metaphysics, who professes to be concerned only with man's earthly destiny, adopts Pascal's notion, but ignores his scale of values: that which in Pascal was mediocrity has now become glory.

It may also be that Vigny's Eva was created out of Pascal's "reasons of the heart which Reason does not recognize." The most important intention of *La Maison du Berger* seems to be to present the figure of the Poet; and this figure is dual in a number of ways: male and female, rational and irrational, altruistic and selfish, sociable and misanthropic, respectable and despicable, idealistic and disillusioned, virtuous and sinful, master and servant of humanity.[25] These dualities become clear from the outset of Part I, in the coupling of the narrator with Eva, in the other notions stated, the style, the arrangement of words.

If your [Eva] heart, groaning under the weight of this life, drags along and struggles like a crippled eagle, bearing, as does mine, a whole fateful, crushing, frozen world upon its enslaved wings, if it beats only as it bleeds from its immortal wound, if it no longer sees love, its faithful star, illuminating for it alone the obliterated horizon . . .[26]

So reads the first stanza. "Eagle," but crippled; "wings," but enslaved; a beating heart pumping blood through an unclosable wound; a heart by which love (of which the heart is the principle) cannot be seen; an imperceptible horizon—in short, so many contradictions in terms. The next two stanzas are no less distressing; they have to do with Eva's soul and with her body, respectively. Her soul, it seems, is a prisoner; her body, subject to "secret passions," wishes (hopefully) to flee the temptations offered it by those who are either unknown or uninitiated or untruthful. We come then to the fourth stanza, which brings the conclusion to the series of conditional clauses which make up the first three: if your heart, soul, and body are as described, then

Depart bravely, leave all the cities behind; don't dirty your feet any longer in the dust of the highways; from the pinnacle of our thoughts look upon the servile cities as the fated rocks of human slavery. The forests and the fields are vast refuges, free as the ocean which surrounds the dark islands. Walk through the fields [countryside] with a flower in your hand.[27]

Seek asylum in Nature, which "awaits you in an austere

silence." There follow (ll. 29–42) two of the finest stanzas in Vigny; the beauty of Nature at sunset and evening twilight is described with a style and a skill reminiscent of, and unsurpassed by, Lamartine, whose *Méditations* are the masterpiece of this sort of thing in French. Unlike Lamartine's, however, Vigny's Nature is part of a purely symbolic scheme. His speaker has already invited Eva to the "pinnacle of our thoughts"; this locality is now described. "There is on my mountain a dense thicket which the hunter's feet enter [only] with difficulty; it raises its lofty head higher than our own, and in the night guards the shepherd and the stranger." [28] We have already noticed Vigny's recurrent use of the shepherd as a figure for the thinker, the interpreter to mankind of the secrets of God and of Nature. Eva is now to come also upon his mountain, there "to hide your love and your divine fault." [29] The meaning of "divine fault" has provoked its share of speculation; upon the scheme which I suggest, attributed to Eva, it seems clearly to refer to the sin of Eve: to assist and stimulate man in the pursuit of the knowledge that God had reserved to himself. Such, in any case, is Eva's function in this poem.

It also seems clear that for Vigny this stimulation is an act of love, and further that the performance of the act must take place in solitude, in freedom from day-to-day existence, away from the "gloomy islands" which are the cities. Ideally, indeed, the agitations and the defects even of Nature will be shut out: "If the foliage [of the thicket] is disturbed, or not high enough, I shall bring there for you the *Maison du Berger*" (the Shepherd's House).[30] This object is not at all Vigny's invention; it was, and is, a sort of caravan or trailer commonly used by herdsmen for shelter and sleeping as they pasture their beasts in the hills during the summer months.[31] The symbol of the shepherd is reinforced, indeed compounded, by the arrangement and the decoration of the shelter:

It moves quietly with its four wheels, its roof is no higher than your eyes, your forehead; the color of coral and that of your cheeks tinge the nocturnal car and its noiseless axles. The threshold is perfumed; the bed-recess is wide and dark, and there, among the flowers, we shall find a silent bed for our mingled hair.[32]

Here will Eva and the narrator consummate their creative union.

[106]

And the character of the creation is indicated in the succeeding stanza:

I shall see, if you wish, the snow countries, those where the amorous star devours and shines, those assaulted by the winds, those besieged by the sea, those where the dark pole is accursed beneath its ice. We shall follow the wandering course of chance. What are daylight or the world to me? I shall say that they are fair when your eyes have told me so.[33]

We notice again that the narrator's vision is directed and qualified by the eyes and the decision of Eva.

The remainder of Part I comprises ten stanzas, all but the last constituting the celebrated diatribe against the railroad. Vigny's treatment, unfortunate or not, fits perfectly, in both purpose and emphasis, into the symbolic scheme of the poem. For it voices the distrust manifested by certain Thinkers in every age, distrust of man's ability to avoid being exploited and destroyed by the natural forces that he has newly and imperfectly bent to his service. In this instance, the force is that of steam; shortly in time the same misgivings will be expressed about electricity, as they are in our time about atomic energy. Jogged by a spectacular French railroad wreck in 1842, which followed closely upon the explosion of an American steamship, and by the well-publicized lawsuits which followed, Vigny, practicing one of his often reiterated notions of poetry, erects the topic into principle and symbol. The fiscal and physical advantages accruing from the harnessing of steam are purchased at the price not only of death and maiming, but also, even more seriously, of the interests of material gain over those of spiritual contemplation.

Yet we must credit to his common sense the fact that Vigny's plea here is not a simple, black-and-white lamentation over matter's defeat of spirit. With some effort, he acknowledges that there are some human values which are well served by the untrustworthy mechanical monster. Our inventiveness has outrun our technological know-how, but at the same time rapid transportation is desirable for such spiritual concerns as the need to defend the fatherland in war and the undoubted duty of a son to arrive in time to close his dying parent's eyes. Barring these, however, "let us avoid those roads"; they are graceless and smoky; one moves over them too rapidly to enjoy and profit from the leisurely contemplation afforded by traditional means of travel; and there is a great risk that all of civilized life will ultimately be ruled by rigid iron rails and timetables.[34] Part I's final stanza states the disastrous consequence:

Never will amorous, peaceful revery see, without horror, its white foot fastened [to cold, silent calculation]; for its eyes must [have leisure to] cast upon every visible object a long gaze, like an overflowing river; it must restlessly interrogate everything; it must, making the divine secrets its concern, walk, stop, and walk again with head bent down.[35]

Apparently it is, or was, difficult to accomplish this on a train.

Revery must not be shackled to technology, or to commerce, or to any other material concern. For Revery is indispensable to Thought, and hence to Thought's distilled expression, which is Poetry. And it is only through Poetry that Man may be able to overcome his destiny.

This last is the burden of Part II. Poetry's sacred function, it seems, has been adulterated in the course of history. The poetic muse has prostituted herself; the semblance of poetry has been made to serve many baser interests (the notion is routine in this and many other periods); and Vigny enumerates a good many of these interests in succeeding stanzas. But man's hope remains solely in the possibility of expressing Thought in works uncontaminated by such gross concerns, works which will outlive their authors and transmit truth to the future. "Poetry, imperishable love of true thinkers," says Vigny,

How would deep thoughts be preserved without bringing together their fires into your pure diamond [this is an interesting and unexplained switch from the "pearl of thought" of line 134] which so well preserves their condensed splendors? that fine mirror, solid, sparkling, and hard, the survivor of dead nations, lasting stone found under one's feet when in the dust one seeks cities without seeing a single wall. Unrivalled diamond, may your fires illuminate the slow, dragging steps of human Reason! The shepherd, in order to see from afar the peoples in their progress, must set you in the roof of his House.[36]

The closing stanzas of Part II contain Vigny's noblest enunciation of his vision of the function of the Poet-*Vates* (they also tend to erase our amusement at his apparent temporizing with technology in Part I):

The day has not yet risen. We are still at [the moment of] the first white ray which precedes the dawn and outlines the earth at the horizon line. The peoples, still in childhood, have scarcely begun to discover one another above the thickets grown up during their sleep, and their hands, reaching through the thornbushes, are making the first arrangement for a mutual grasp. Barbarity still holds our feet in its sheath. The marble of the old times immobilizes us to our waist, and every energetic man is like the god Terminus. But our rapid mind is abundant in movement; let us open the whole arsenal of its powerful springs. The invisible is real. Souls have their own world in which impalpable treasures are piled up. The Lord contains everything in his two immense arms, his Word is the abiding-place of our intelligences, as the space on earth is that of our bodies.[37]

Poetry is the triumph of Man. The greatest of Men is the Poet. The Poet is not simply a man, but a male-female duality. And the female element is as indispensable to this being as is the male. This much is clear in *La Maison du Berger* above all; it is unmistakable in many other items in this book.

In the collection *Les Destinées,* Eva herself figures also in *Les Oracles* and in *L'Esprit pur.* In two others, *La Sauvage* and *Wanda,* the female element is predominantly stressed. Neither of these poems has been much admired by posterity, no doubt because they are routine expressions of hackneyed ideas. Let us say merely that the Russian princess Wanda, who lives out her life with her children and her arbitrarily condemned husband in the mines of Siberia, and the unnamed American Indian woman, driven by the murderous Hurons to seek shelter for herself and her children with the family of the blond Anglo-Saxon pioneer—each of these in her way represents an element without which civilization cannot be realized. Each, that is, is a fragmentary counterpart of Eva. The fabled nobility of Vigny's wolf (*La Mort du loup*) exists because of the presence of his mate and his cubs. Samson's Dalila might be called an exception to the rule for Vigny's females. More exactly, perhaps, she is to be seen as the female accompaniment to one of the two heroes in the collection (the other is the Jesus of *Le Mont des oliviers*) who fail to recognize the fact that their strength belongs to their humanity and does not depend upon the pronunciation of some shibboleth. Dalila's domination of Samson is explicitly made possible by Samson's will, or knowing lack of will.

Of the eleven poems in *Les Destinées,* in other words, seven give extraordinary importance to essentially similar female roles. While there is surely nothing more common in any period than the poet's claim to find in his ladylove the inspiration for his art, yet Vigny's insistent, detailed attribution to the female of a complex transcendental function indispensable to the high public mission of artistic creation is unexampled, I believe, in French Romantic poetry—excepting only Baudelaire's incomparably richer performance in *Les Fleurs du mal* (1857), of which, by the way, Vigny did not approve.[38]

For all that, Woman does not appear in *La Flûte* or in *La Bouteille à la mer,* and in the "person" of Eva, her role in *L'Esprit pur* is that of passive addressee. In these three, however, it seems logical not to find her. They are concerned with the effects of the Poet's work, not with its origins.

La Flûte is another variation on a favorite theme: the unheeded, thus unsuccessful, artist. In this case, his failure with the public has made him lose confidence in his talent and in his mission. He cannot, moreover, produce in fact the music that he has imagined. The sympathetically understanding narrator assures him that the defects in his performance are to be attributed to the imperfection of his instrument; his lack of public success comes from the public's customary obtuseness. Let him, in short, cheer up; no artist satisfactorily realizes his talents in this life:

Your breath was exact and your song is off key. For me, who know nothing and who go from doubt to dream, I think that after death, when union is finally accomplished, the soul finds vision and light; that [the soul], judging its work with serenity, understanding without hindrance and explaining itself without difficulty, . . . measures itself by a true standard, visibly recognizes that its breath was made false by the false instrument, that [its breath] was neither glorious nor vile, since it was not free; that it was the body solely which hindered its rightness; and then, calm, [the soul] resumes, in ideal happiness, the holy balance of the spirits of the Lord.[39]

This sage commentary immeasurably encourages the poor flute-player, who resumes his tootling: "The pitch was truer and the breath unfaltering." [40]

This poem is competently versified in 140 Alexandrines. Its

theme and its treatment are very routine; and for at least one present-day reader the patronizing attitude of the narrator toward the artist (a trait not shown in the selections quoted) is distasteful (one feels that both of them should have known better). But for all that, the poem is not the defense of artistic ineptitude that existing critical tradition has made of it.[41] It is, on the contrary, despite its condescension, another consistent item in the poetical gospel according to Vigny. For this reason alone I mention here more than its title.

The remaining items in *Les Destinées*, that is to say *La Bouteille à la mer* and *L'Esprit pur*, are major ones in length and in popularity; they are very competently made; they are eloquent (and possibly unnecessary) reiterations of Vigny's perennial notion of the Poet's sacrifice and its ultimately beneficial effects upon posterity and his own vanity. Since the two poems are so famous, I think it necessary to summarize them; since they are so ordinary, I think that I need here supply no more than a summary of them.

La Bouteille à la mer, then, somewhat pretentiously subtitled "Advice to an unknown young man," comprises 182 Alexandrines in the seven-line stanza that I have previously mentioned.[42] In the first stanza the young man is urged to "forget the children interrupted by death," among them the Chatterton and the Gilbert previously exploited by Vigny in *Stello* and in his play; "[having become] piously idolatrous of the future, finally, forget the man in yourself.—Listen." [43] No longer the poet, in short, but his work and its effects. Follows a fable: a "grave mariner," his ship about to founder in perilous seas, encloses the results of his scientific investigations in an empty champagne bottle, corks it well, and throws it overboard. He goes down with his ship. The bottle, having undergone vicissitudes commensurate with its journey from somewhere south and west of Cape Horn, is finally pulled in by a Breton fisherman, who rushes its contents to the nearest "savant," and a national celebration sets in. Knowledge, despite all, has come home; in a gesture of defiance at the tale of original sin, Vigny concludes his poem:

The tree of greatness grows over the stone of the dead. This tree is the fairest in the promised land. It is the beacon of all of you, hard-working Thinkers! . . . The true God, the strong God, is the God of ideas.[44]

The immortality owing to the discoverer of knowledge is declared in *L'Esprit pur*, the last poem in the collection and presumably the poet's farewell statement to his public. Once again he uses seven-line stanzas, ten of them, in the *ababccb* rhyme scheme previously noted. This address to Eva is an elaboration on two themes: the poet's noble heritage, and the glory which he alone has brought upon it. Both are enunciated in the first stanza:

If pride seizes upon your heart when the public pronounces my name, let your pride come only from my books; upon the gilded crest of the gentleman I have affixed a plume [in French a pun on pen] of iron which does not lack beauty. I have made illustrious a name transmitted to me without glory. Though it is ancient, it will be memorable only from the day when it has been borne by me.[45]

There follow six stanzas describing the routinely noble activities of the poet's routinely noble ancestors, concluding:

All of them died, leaving their name without a halo; but now it is written on the golden disk: "Here passed two races of Gaul, whose last survivor mounts to the temple and there writes himself down, not upon the obscure collection of the old, useless names of the malicious proud and the futile rich, but upon the pure roll of the titles of the MIND."[46]

He goes on (Stanza VIII) to announce the advent of the reign of the Mind, which has displaced that of war; he even implies that Mind's accession to kingship (Vigny's figure) constitutes the arrival of the millennium. The title to nobility under this new regime is the written work,

THE UNIVERSAL WRITING, sometimes imperishable, which you [Mind] engrave on marble or drag across the sand, dove with a beak of bronze! VISIBLE HOLY SPIRIT![47]
I remain, the single, last link of two broken chains. And I uphold still in the heights, among the pure masters in our learned museums, the IDEAL of the poet and of the serious thinkers. I have tested its duration in twenty years of silence, and still, and from age to age, I see France looking at my works and casting flowers upon them.[48]

The final stanza envisages his survival in the works of those who come after him.

Young posterity of a living man who loves you! My features are not erased in your eyes; in this mirror I can *recognize myself*, [this mirror which is] an eternally new judge of our past works! Ever-reborn waves of friends! May my destinies[49] bring you to me from decade to decade, [may you be] attentive to my work, and for me this is enough![50]

The passage is a beautiful one, full of nobility and pride, and also of humility. It is a very fitting conclusion, I think, to the work of this strange, disdainful, pathetic, exasperating, exalted, and curiously fascinating man. It is dated March 10, 1863. Vigny died on September 16.

III   Servitude et grandeur militaires

The "immortality" that Vigny was so confident of having earned is, after all, only a century old; it was not very apparent, moreover, in the period between his death and the resurgence of interest in him which began in the 1920's. Such as it is, it rests, as has been said, almost entirely upon some of his verse. Perhaps one should add *Chatterton*, which, however, is less a good play than it is a period piece and an interesting historical phenomenon. There remains *Servitude et grandeur militaires*. One may pardonably guess that within the next century the name of Vigny will suggest *Servitude* even sooner than it does any of his verse.

Servitude's destiny up to now has been peculiar. It has been valued as a class text, to be sure; otherwise, it is the agonies of France in three disastrous wars which have made its success. As an exposition of the cult of honor, as a tribute to the self-sacrificing humility of the modern soldier, it is unsurpassed, indeed unequalled, in French literature. It was edited in part, for example, some twenty years ago by no less a personage than Charles de Gaulle.[51] In its career it has fulfilled the same function as did the Roman plays of Corneille during the Revolution and the First Empire. It has been used, that is, almost exclusively as an unexceptionable piece of patriotic propaganda. Its literary merits have by no means been ignored, but they have been subordinated to extra-literary concerns.

Servitude is undeniably a work of patriotism, but its understanding of this quality is much broader and deeper than that accorded it by many of us today. We recall that the three stories were written in a period when the royalist Vigny was considerably disillusioned with French royalty, with both the authoritarian stupidities of Charles X and the unglamorous bourgeoisie of Louis-Philippe. The manner and method of these tales amply testifies to their author's painful situation: that of the extraordinary soldier who gives his first and undeviating loyalty in his actions to the ruling regime, while he is nonetheless largely disenchanted with the persons, the policies, and even the legitimacy of the regime. His only refuge, the only possible salvation of his conscience, lies in thoroughly carrying out his orders and at the same time in a gnawing, burning remorse at the consequences of his activities. In other words, the soldier is at once a person and an unquestioning instrument of authority, and the claims of these two conditions poignantly conflict within him.

The theme, of course, is as old as the *res publica*. The principal merits of Vigny's treatment are two: (1) His solution to the dilemma: by carrying out his duty and suffering his remorse, the soldier keeps his conscience clear, being thus assured of his dignity as a human being—he belongs to that active company who alone among persons deserve the title of *man*. (2) The unusual (for Vigny) intensity of feeling which pervades these stories, together with the restrained sobriety of their style. One is reminded of much of Racine's theater: here is almost no oratory or prettiness, still less any flamboyance. The language is the most ordinary, the most colloquial, in Vigny. The words, the lines, are simple, quiet, almost monotonous; it is what they say that screams, and the scream is all the more heart-rending for the quietness of its expression.

To account to some extent for this achievement, let us remember that before Vigny was a poet, he was a soldier. Ever-mindful of the military origins of the hereditary nobility, he always saw himself as being by race a knightly *comes;* in habitually styling himself *comte* Alfred de Vigny he did far more than claim a merely contemporary social distinction.

Upon this familial tradition was laid a career of thirteen years as a professional soldier, a period which was undoubtedly the most contented of his life. Never an enlisted man, never engaged in combat, he began his army service in 1814 and terminated it in 1827. From first to last he was on garrison assignments, and he spent the larger part of the last five years on leave. There was no glory in his military career, nor did he ever pretend that there was. But, even discounting his extensive leave time, eight years of active service is an ample lapse in which to become thoroughly acquainted with the realities of army life, above all with the monotonous routine which is its most distinctive quality. The monotony is bad enough in time of war; it must be greatly intensified in a period when there is no war nor any apparent threat of war. In such a situation, one soon learns one's professional functions so completely that they become automatic, to the point where the slightest variation in routine constitutes an adventure. And then one has time for thought, if monotony has not killed the desire for it; one spends incalculable hours in talk; most important of all, perhaps (and in Vigny's case this seems a certainty), one is compelled to live closely with a very heterogeneous assemblage of other men, and, to the extent that one is at all perceptive, to learn in detail their realities with a thoroughness scarcely to be achieved in any other kind of existence. The thing that Vigny knew best all his life long as a matter of real experience was the peacetime army of his term of service. His knowledge of it was masterful. This mastery is splendidly put to work in *Servitude*.

The work comprises three short stories, each prefaced by a philosophical, or, more properly, moralizing essay. The tales were first published separately in the *Revue des deux mondes*, one each in 1833, 1834, and 1835. In 1835 also they were published together as a book under their present collective title. The first two, *Laurette ou le cachet rouge* and *La Veillée de Vincennes*, are grouped under the heading *Souvenirs de servitude militaire;* the third, *La Canne de jonc*, otherwise *La Vie et la mort du capitaine Renaud*, is headed *Souvenirs de grandeur militaire*. The latter rubric implies an intention to add other tales, and Vigny's journal contains a number of suggestions and plans which he apparently did not carry out.[52]

His failure to do so is regrettable. Nowhere else in his work, not even in his journal or in his correspondence, does he give so completely the impression of speaking the language of common humanity. Nowhere else does he seem to write so unaffectedly, with such a lack of gentlemanly self-consciousness. No other of his works speaks so directly to the general reader.

To this reader, at least, this appearance of unstylized naturalness indicates a very high order of artistic achievement. Compared to the style of the narrator and of the speakers in these stories, the speech indited by such self-conscious realists as Balzac or Dickens sounds insufferably stilted or caricatural. My point is not that convincing realism is the *sine qua non* of artistry, but rather that genuine artistry must be founded upon knowledge so intimate as to have become as it were instinctive, and that the artist must have the talent to express this knowledge in such a way as to seduce his reader into wholehearted acquiescence, no matter how stylized or artificial (or naturalistic) the form of expression. One is so seduced, I take it, by Homer and Dante and Chaucer and Milton (at least by certain passages of them), by much of Shakespeare, most of Molière, Jane Austen, Melville, Baudelaire, Dostoevsky, Whitman, Joyce, Proust, Eliot, Frost, Pirandello, Brecht, Camus. *Servitude* operates such a seduction, I think; in Vigny's case, this achievement is owing in large measure to the perfection of a "natural" style which does not exist elsewhere in his writings. His soldiers and his sailors, his officers and his enlisted men in the infantry, the artillery, and the elite corps, the veterans of the Revolution and of the Napoleonic campaigns, the young men of the Restoration army, the disillusioned "retreads" of the reign of Louis-Philippe—each of these speaks a language of his own which seems, at least at this distance, to be perfectly appropriate to his service and to his station, and to the situation of the moment. *Servitude,* I repeat, is unique in the Vigny canon as being the one work in which Thought is founded upon exhaustive, real knowledge.

It is the Thought which interests us here. Vigny presents the three tales as actual personal reminiscences of episodes either narrated to him or participated in by him in the course of his military exertions. Looking back upon his army career some six years after it had ended, Vigny has come to visualize the Soldier and his relationships to the rest of society as being analogous in some important respects to the Poet. The first paragraph of the conclusion appended to *La Canne de jonc* is explicit:

The period which left me these scattered memories is closed today. Its circle opened in 1814 with the battle of Paris, and closed with the three days of Paris in 1830. This was the time in which, as I have said, the army of the Empire was coming to die in the bosom of the army then aborning, and mature today. Having, under various forms, explained the nature and pitied the situation of the Poet in our society, I have tried here to show that of the Soldier, another modern Pariah.[53]

The irony is evident: both pariahs are entirely given over to the service of society; both are misunderstood, denigrated, cast out. Both lead an existence quite alien to that of the rest of society, and both find their ultimate dignity in the utter abnegation of their personal interests for the benefit of society.

There is one outstanding distinction between the two: the Soldier's abnegation consists in unquestioning obedience to the will of his government, however misguided that may be in fact or in his opinion. The Poet's, on the other hand, consists in taking the ostracizing consequences of his absolute refusal to bow to established authority, be it religious, philosophical, moral, political, social, economic, or other. The Soldier has a fixed place in a hierarchy of discipline, absolute authority over his subordinates, absolute subjection to his superiors, who themselves are in the same situation; responsibility thus resides only in the commander-in-chief; and a soldier's excellence, in his own and in others' eyes, depends upon his unqualified acceptance of this condition. He is therefore, in Vigny's phrase, "proud to be in no way responsible." [54] The Poet's responsibility, on the other hand, as we have seen in the *Chatterton* of the same 1835, goes beyond the ultimate; it is he who must guide the commander-in-chief.

Servitude and Grandeur—Poet and Soldier alike are subject to both conditions. Servitude is exemplified in the first two stories. *Laurette* is the distressing tale of three people: a ship commander in the service of the Directoire, and a young couple. The captain is under orders to transport the young man to the penal colony in French Guiana; the young man's bride goes along. The captain has additional, sealed orders which he must open only upon reaching a specified latitude and longitude in his crossing. Before arriving at this location, he has become very affectionately disposed toward the young people, to the extent of looking upon them as his adopted children; beyond this, he plans to quit the service and to live with them in Guiana. The sealed orders, duly opened, command the young man's immediate execution. The captain obeys forthwith. Despite his precautions, the wife witnesses the event, and goes quietly mad. The captain takes her under his protection, returns to France, leaves the navy, joins the army, takes her everywhere with him in a cart, rises to the rank of major in the army of the Empire, and dies at Waterloo. Laurette, transported to hospital, dies a few days thereafter. Duty to his superiors, duty to their (and his) victim—both are unquestioningly fulfilled in the most difficult circumstances.

The young man's crime having been simply the publication of some verses critical of the Directors, the captain finds the severity of his punishment whimsical, to say the least. He nonetheless inflicts it without hesitation and also without supervision. There is no commissar aboard his ship, and he could undoubtedly find some way to evade carrying out his orders, be humanly decent, and get away with it. But the thought never occurs to him, nor does it, apparently, to Vigny. The captain is very literally the slave of duty.[55]

The second story, *La Veillée de Vincennes*, presents another slave. The duty is somewhat different, being that of a garrison soldier preparing for a royal inspection. The soldier is a sergeant-major (*adjudant*) of artillery whose specific job consists in making sure that the munitions on hand check accurately against the paper accounts thereof. The inspection is to take place early in the morning; the hero is first shown us at twilight of the day before, repeatedly verifying his records and worrying because regulations forbid his entering the magazine after dark, since the necessary lantern would cause the intolerable risk of explosion. The explosion duly takes place, between midnight and dawn, causing the fragmentation of the overconscientious hero, some of whose pieces are identified by the narrator and some of his fellow officers who have dutifully rushed to their perilous posts immediately after the cataclysm.

This rather silly framework encloses a beautifully wrought pastiche of a rococo operetta which has nothing to do with military servitude. Instead, we get a Romantic royalist's sentimental evocation of Marie-Antoinette as the delicately capricious milkmaid queen; having accidentally encountered a peasant lad and his lass, she is so taken with the latter's costume that she arranges to exchange clothing with her, and subsequently rewards the two by sending the lad into the army and enabling the lass to earn her dowry by a single performance as the heroine of the operetta *Rose et Colas* (music by Monsigny, words by the lad's old friend Sedaine). It is the sergeant-major, formerly the peasant lad, who tells this tale within a tale shortly before his ultimate trip to the magazine; his hero is Sedaine.

Sedaine was in fact that rarity among prominent literary figures, one who over a considerable period of time earned his keep by hard physical labor; he was a stonemason. He wrote a number of libretti which were extremely popular in his time. Most important of all, he wrote the finest bourgeois drama in French before *Chatterton*: *Le Philosophe sans le savoir* (1765). Unlike that of *Chatterton,* this play's intention is to justify the businessman in the face of aristocratic snobbery. And also unlike the businessmen and the snobs of *Chatterton,* Sedaine's hero has a heart, and his actions are guided by it. It is presumably for this reason that Vigny chooses his predecessor as a sort of hero. At any rate, he presents Sedaine as the poet, or, more exactly, as the impresario who operates, through a fairy-tale queen, the realization of love's young dream.

All of this means that *La Veillée de Vincennes,* apart from its inept framework (which may be truth, but which is not very good fiction), does not fit very well into the solemn scheme of *Servitude.* It is nevertheless a charming story charmingly told. It does not defend any thesis or illustrate any well-defined principle. Apart from its presentation of Sedaine, it seems to exist for its own sake as a competently made piece of stylized fiction. The sergeant-major's "servitude" and Sedaine's role are too superficial for us to look upon them as being serious attempts to convey a message.

La Canne de jonc, on the other hand, is very serious indeed. It is also, at least to some of us, the best piece of prose to come from Vigny's pen. Beside its two companion stories it stands somewhat as does Beethoven's third symphony in comparison to his first and second symphonies. That is to say that while the first two are excellently well-crafted, the third is far more complicated, subtle, and profound.

Most of the story is related by its hero, Captain Renaud, an army officer whom the original narrator (or author) encounters commanding a Paris barricade on one of the three July nights of the 1830 revolution. This is a man whose soldier-father had taken him, still a child, on Napoleon's expedition to Egypt, and who, before being sent back with other dependents from Malta, had been lifted up and kissed by the future emperor, who promised his father to make a good soldier of him.

I felt that he was my master and that he was taking my soul away from my father. . . . I thought I was experiencing the fright of Moses, the shepherd, seeing God in the burning bush. Bonaparte had picked me up free, and when his arms put me down again upon the deck, they left there an additional slave.[56]

Henceforth Renaud is devoted to a man, Napoleon. In due course he becomes a lieutenant. Assigned to the forces which are to feign a cross-channel invasion of England, he is captured by an English vessel, and spends an unspecified number of years as a prisoner. For good fictional reasons he is adopted by the English Admiral Collingwood (this tale's second hero), whose destiny is to remain forever at sea in the blockade of the Continent. From the admiral he learns the distinction between devotion to a man and devotion to a principle.

The sight of this true citizen devoted, not as I had been, to a man, but to the Fatherland and to Duty, was a fortunate happening for me, for I learned, in this severe school, what is the veritable Grandeur that we must henceforth seek for in the profession of arms, and how high, when [this grandeur] is thus understood, it raises our profession above all the others. . . . Never did any man possess to a higher degree the inner peace born of the feeling of sacred Duty, and the modest freedom from care of a soldier to whom personal fame matters little, provided that the welfare of his nation prosper.[57]

Vigny's term for this devotion is Honor, and Honor equals Grandeur. But Honor's or Grandeur's necessary disregard for persons raises an uncomfortable problem, essentially the same as the one faced by the major in *Laurette*: inevitably one encounters a situation in which Honor's demands conflict with the ordinary claims of respect and decency made upon one human being by the existence of another. The knowledge that one has preferred Honor over persons does nothing to lessen the horror which comes from inflicting injury or death upon another person, especially if that person is defenseless. Captain Renaud has found himself so horrified, so agonized. Having been ordered to lead a night attack on a Russian outpost on the perimeter of Rheims, he and his men find the Russians asleep in their darkened barracks; the attack is successful, and the slaughter complete.

On entering, I had struck at random a terrific blow against something black that I had pierced through and through; an old officer, a tall, heavy man, his head covered with white hair, rose up like a ghost, gave a frightful cry as he saw what I had done, struck me violently in the face with his sword, and instantly fell dead under the bayonets. I fell beside him in a sitting position, stunned by the blow between the eyes, and I heard beneath me the dying and tender voice of a child saying: "Papa . . ."

Then I understood what I had done. . . . I saw one of those fourteen-year-old officers who were so numerous in the Russian armies sent against us at that time.[58]

Follows the description of an angelic child with the captain's saber through his heart. And then the captain's colonel arrives with congratulations for his successful attack:

"Look at that," I said; "what's the difference between me and a murderer?"

"Oh, hell, old man, what of it? It's part of the job."

"You're right," I replied, and I got up to resume my command. The child fell back into his cloak, and I wrapped him in it, and his little hand . . . let fall a malacca cane, which fell upon my hand as if he had given it to me. I took it; I made up my mind never to carry any other weapon, no matter what dangers I might encounter, and I had not the courage to withdraw my murderous sabre from his body.[59]

The captain keeps this promise, survives the army of the Empire, takes service with the Restoration army, retires on schedule shortly previous to the July troubles. When these occur, he comes out of retirement to serve once again. Soon after telling his story, he is shot by a drunken juvenile unaware, at the moment, of what he is doing and why he is doing it. Having sobered up, he is conscience-stricken, and serves the captain as best he can during the few days it takes the old soldier to die of gangrene. The captain, ever mindful of the Russian child, finds satisfaction and peace in the manner of his death. He has somehow paid his personal debt to the Russian child. He has moreover voluntarily put on the uniform which procured his death;

his duty is to the army, despite his personal disapproval of the regime commanding the army. Honor has brought him back to the service of a cause whose legitimacy was not altered by its unpopularity.[60]

In the context of the whole of this tale, its most famous episode is merely incidental. Since it is famous, however, we had better notice it. The child kissed by Napoleon at Malta becomes a page to the emperor. As such he witnesses, concealed, an interview between Napoleon and the pope, Pius VII, which takes place when the latter arrives, a virtual prisoner, at Fontainebleau.[61] The frail old pope is confronted, cajoled, threatened, and otherwise browbeaten by the young and powerful ruler, whose leading characteristic, in this chapter, at least, is verbosity. Vigny nails down the contrast between the two, and also the moral victory of the representative of matters spiritual, by making the pope win the debate by pronouncing only two words. The chapter is picturesque, even dramatic; it is quite unhistorical. Its only justification is its contribution to Renaud's awareness of the superiority of spiritual values over those of force.

But what are spiritual values? They were hard to define in France in the 1830's (as they have been and are in other times and places). The consecrated notions of throne and religion now seemed to be no more than convenient masks for ambition, venality, and weakness. God and the monarchy were moribund, if not already dead. One's overpowering need for some certainty, some faith, could not be satisfied by them. The confused welter of values of all sorts in a civilization in painful transition was driving the Thinker to seize upon the only immaterial certainty, the only spirituality that he could count upon—his own. Unlike the Vigny of *Les Destinées*, the Vigny of the 1830's still needed to attach his devotion to some extra-personal concept.

In the universal shipwreck of beliefs, what pieces remain for generous hands to cling to? Apart from the love of well-being and current luxury, nothing can be seen floating on the surface of the abyss. One would think that egotism has submerged everything; the very persons who seek to save souls and who dive in courageously feel themselves threatened with being swallowed up. The leaders of the political parties today take Catholicism as a catchword and a banner; but what faith have they in its marvels, and how do they follow its law in their own lives? The artists exhibit it as though it were a precious medallion, and plunge into its dogmas as into an epic source of poetry; but how many of them are there who kneel down in the church which they decorate? Many philosophers are embracing and pleading its cause, as generous lawyers do that of a poor and neglected client; their writings and their words are fond of taking on its colors and its forms, they like to decorate their books with its gothic gildings, their whole work complacently twists about its cross the clever labyrinth of their arguments; but it is rare that that cross is beside them when they are alone. The men of war command and die almost without remembering God. Our Age knows that it is this way; it would like to be otherwise, and it cannot be so. It looks upon itself with a gloomy eye, and no other age has felt more keenly how unhappy it is to be an age which sees itself.[62]

And so, says Vigny in this concluding chapter of *La Canne de jonc,* I have sought and finally found, although with some uncertainty, "a point . . . strong enough to serve as a support in the tempest, and I have been reassured." He goes on to speak of it:

It is not a new faith, a newly invented cult, a vague thought; it is a feeling born with us, independent of times, places, and even of religions; a feeling which is proud, inflexible, an incomparably beautiful instinct, which has not found in modern times a name worthy of it, but which was already producing sublime grandeurs in antiquity. . . . This faith, which seems to me still to be possessed by everyone and to reign supremely in the Armies, is that of HONOR.[63]

The Thinker does not write very clearly. He tells us that Honor is a feeling, an instinct; he implies that it is a faith, a cult, a thought; and then he turns it into a virtue. But if this way of writing is unclear, it is at least convenient, convenient above all for the making of images as distinguished from concepts. However philosophically vague Vigny's Honor may be, he leaves us not in the slightest doubt in human terms as to what he is talking about.

An indefinable vitality animates this queer, proud virtue, which holds itself erect in the midst of all our vices, even agreeing with them to the point of enhancing itself with their energy. While all the virtues seem to come down from heaven to give us their hand and raise us up, this one [Honor] seems to come *from ourselves* and to tend to rise to heaven. It is an altogether *human* virtue, which may be thought to be born of *earth,* with no celestial palm after death; *it is the virtue of life.*[64]

Man's only certainty is Honor, which originates within man himself. We have nearly arrived, in other words, at the utter humanism of *Les Destinées,* particularly as it is illustrated in *La Maison du Berger.* Recalling the Eva of that poem, let us listen to one more passage in the conclusion of *Servitude et grandeur militaires:*

> Man, at the name of Honor, feels stirring in him something which is like a part of himself, and this stimulus awakens all the strength of his pride and of his primeval energy. An unconquerable firmness sustains him against everyone and against himself at the thought of watching over the pure tabernacle which is in his bosom like a second heart in which resides a god. From this there come to him inner consolations which are all the more beautiful because he does not know their true source, their true cause; from this also [there come] sudden revelations of the True, the Beautiful, the Just; from this, a light which goes before him.
> Honor is conscience, but conscience exalted. It is respect for oneself and for the beauty of one's life carried to the purest elevation and to the most burning passion.[65]

The undoubted nobility of this notion and the eloquence of its expression may obscure its vagueness and its pessimism, but they do not alter them. And its essential despair is not alleviated for being beautifully expressed. The man who, like so many of us, needs, seeks, even cries out for a god to worship, and who finds at the end of his quest no more than himself—this is a disappointed, perhaps frustrated, and surely fearful man, who may be forgiven if he adopts either the attitude of iconoclastic rebellion or that of the aloof and disdainful martyr (there are of course other possibilities). Such in general were the situation of the Romantics and the faces which they put upon it. Vigny invariably chose the role of impassive martyr, as both *Servitude* and all the rest of his work make plain.

Servitude et grandeur militaires functions, so to speak, as the key to Vigny the writer. Into itself it gathers all the themes and practices of his past; it distils and transforms them, and incubates, as it were, and implies the remaining and supreme fragment of his work, which is *Les Destinées.*

CHAPTER 4

Conclusion

IT is not difficult to see in Vigny the theorist and practitioner of poetry a notable precursor of most of the notable poets who have followed him. Poets, earnest ones at least, usually seem to believe in the poet-*vates* notion. Somewhat more specifically, Vigny's disillusionment with God and king, his skepticism with respect to metaphysical and traditional values, his ultimate faith placed solely in his own intelligent humanity—these things are prominent in most of the artists and the artistic isms between his time and ours. Here, but with varying individual colorations, are Baudelaire, Gautier, Leconte de l'Isle, Mallarmé, Valéry, St. Exupéry, and Camus (and I name only poets). As we, from our moment in time and civilization, are able to look back and to distinguish the principal monuments in the history of poetry and of poetic ideas, we discern in Vigny an entity considerably greater, more fertile, than Hugo or Lamartine or Musset. Between the splendidly original and skillful Chénier and the giant that was Baudelaire, it is Vigny who overtops the rest, who appears first to the eyes and the spirit and the understanding of our generation.

What did his surviving contemporaries make of him? Surely they had no more sensitive, nor more articulate a spokesman than Théophile Gautier. Twelve days after the Thinker's death, Gautier, whose poetic theories and practices were far removed from Vigny's, published a memorial to him in his column in *Le Moniteur*; it reads in part as follows:

Few writers have brought to life as did Alfred de Vigny the ideal image that one conceives of a poet. Of noble birth, bearing a name as melodious as the vibration of a lyre, having a seraphic beauty which, even in the last days of his life neither age nor sufferings had been able to alter, sufficiently well off so that no vulgar necessity forced him into miserable daily tasks, he kept his literary countenance pure, calm, poetic. He was indeed the poet of Eloa, the virgin, born of a tear of the Christ, who out of pity went down to console Lucifer. Vigny alone, even among that constellation of poets sparkling in the sky, could have written this poem, the most beautiful, perhaps the most perfect one in the French language. He alone possessed those pearly greys, those reflections of iridescence,[1] those opal-like transparencies, that moonlight blue, which are capable of making the immaterial discernible against the white background of the light of heaven. The present generation seems to have forgotten *Eloa*. It is rarely spoken of or cited. It is nonetheless a priceless jewel to be set in the golden doors of the tabernacle . . .

When one thinks of Vigny, one involuntarily imagines him as a swan swimming with his neck curved back a little, his wings slightly filled with the breeze, on one of the transparent and bejeweled ponds of the English parks, a *Virginia Water* scratched by a moonbeam falling through the sea-green tresses of the willows. He is a whiteness in a ray of light, a silver track upon a limpid mirror, a sigh among water flowers and pale foliage. He can also be compared to one of those nebulous drops of milk upon the blue bosom of the sky, which shine less brightly than the other stars because they are placed higher and farther away.[2]

This passage, in a manner quite alien to Vigny's (for example, it contains more shades of color than are to be found in the whole of Vigny's work), is perhaps a better poem than any its subject ever wrote. Lest my skeptical reader conclude that Gautier is being merely guilty of outrageous Victorian insipidity, let me assure him that, on the contrary, by the use of currently fashionable symbols—blue, irridescence, grey, white, transparency, light, mirror, swan, star, jewel, nebulosity, etc.—Gautier has crammed a wealth of critical perception into an extremely small package. His evaluation boils down to the idealism, the disinterestedness, the purity, the integrity, the "exile," and the obsession with the poet's mission which characterize both Vigny and his work. Perhaps unwittingly, it also conveys a hint of that work's superficiality.

As for Vigny in our own day, the foregoing pages try to indicate something of a twentieth-century judgment of him; beyond that, they attempt to furnish their reader with sufficient materials for the making of his own judgment. Vigny, in any case, rightly or wrongly, spent his maturity looking upon himself as the misunderstood, vilified, devoted servant of uncomprehending humanity, a sorrowful man not unacquainted with grief. And when the bruises and the stripes requisite for the rest of the role were not spontaneously forthcoming, on occasion he went out of his way to provoke them.[3]

By family heritage, by intellectual conviction, and also, in many of his activities, actually the dedicated servant of humanity, he disdained the humanity that he existed to serve. And when it repaid him in kind, he made of himself an altered Christ. Nothing could be more Romantic; nothing could be more banal. And yet, with all this against him, Vigny is not, as he so often deserves to be, ridiculous. For his ludicrous pretensions, like the rest of them, are founded upon a real nobility of spirit, and expressed in some of the finest pages in French literature.

Notes and References

Chapter One

1. All translations from French in this book are my own.

2. Victor Hugo, *Oeuvres complètes,* edition *Ne Varietur* (Paris, n. d.), I, 5. The passage is tricky to translate: "L'histoire des hommes ne présente de poésie que jugée du haut des idées monarchiques et des croyances religieuses."

3. *Ibid.,* pp. 6-7.

4. *Ibid.,* pp. 16-17. Emphasis added.

5. *Ibid.,* pp. 20-21.

6. I know of no good general study in English of French Romanticism.

7. See Lester G. Crocker, *An Age of Crisis; Man and World in Eighteenth Century French Thought* (Baltimore, 1959).

8. Genoude, in *Le Conservateur,* March 1820, quoted by R. Bray, *Chronologie du romantisme* (Paris, 1932), p. 47.

9. Bray, *op. cit.,* pp. 70-71.

Chapter Two

1. The most convenient repository of Vigny's works today is his *Oeuvres complètes,* edited by F. Baldensperger, published by Gallimard in *Bibliothèque de la Pléiade* (Paris, 1950), 2 vols. This edition underwent a second printing in 1955, in the course of which some changes were made in pagination. References to Vigny's work in the present book identified simply by volume and page numbers are to the 1955 printing of this edition. The edition contains numerous misprints; its arrangement, moreover, is cumbersome, and sometimes mystifying, particularly to the nonspecialist.

2. The text of the journal in the *Pléiade* edition is considerably supplemented in Alfred de Vigny, *Mémoires inédits; fragments et projets,* ed. Jean Sangnier (Paris, 1958).

3. See letter published by Ernest Dupuy in *La Jeunesse des Romantiques* (Paris, 1905), p. 220.

4. E. g., *Journal d'un poète,* May 14, 1832: "There is but one motto for all journals. I have never in my life read one which was not subject to it: mediocrity, mendacity, malice.

The mass of people being mediocre, mendacious, and malicious, is fond of journals. This was to be expected" (II, 958).

5. *Journal d'un poète,* 1824, II, 880.

6. *Oeuvres complètes,* II, 723-25.

7. If Vigny indentifies the statue of Memnon, it is not unlikely that he wishes to remind his reader that its famous ability to speak resulted from a trick of construction which caused it to make a noise in the warmth of the rising sun. In other words, the principle of the statue's speech lay outside it, not within it; the statue was nothing more than a mechanism by which a universal inspiration was momentarily particularized.

8. II, 732-33.

9. II, 733-34.

10. II, 750-51.

11. II, 735.

12. II, 749.

13. *Ibid.*

14. II, 750.

15. Blue is a standard symbol for ideality, constantly so used by Vigny, and in nineteenth-century French literature in general.

16. II, 735.

17. II, 736.

18. II, 745.

19. P. Bonnefoy, *La Pensée religieuse et morale d'Alfred de Vigny* (Paris, n. d. [1946]), Part I, ch. 5. In my opinion this is the most sensitive and the best written book in the bibliography of Vigny studies.

20. II, 747.

21. II, 20.

22. II, 21.

23. *Ibid.*

24. II, 22.

25. II, 25.

26. II, 266.

27. II, 269.

28. II, 163.

29. II, 240-41.

30. II, 241-42.

31. II, 330.

32. Vigny assigns to his poems some dates of composition which are open to question. The purposes of the present study are not such as to justify detailed investigation into this matter.

33. All biblical quotations in English are from the King James version.

34. II, 139-40:
Semblaient chercher encore quelqu'autre dans ces lieux. All ref-

erences to *Poèmes antiques et modernes* are to the critical edition of them published by E. Estève (*Société des textes français modernes*) (Paris, 1931).

35. ll. 50-54:
Et la première aurore est son premier supplice:
Elle vit tout ensemble et la faute et le lieu,
S'étonna d'elle-même et douta de son Dieu.
Elle joignit les mains.

36. ll. 57-68.

37. ll. 61-64:
Elle voulut, bravant la céleste défense,
Voir une fois encor les lieux de son enfance,
Ou peut-être, écoutant un coeur ambitieux,
Surprendre d'un regard le grand secret des cieux.

38. l. 76:
Mais l'époux, dans le fils, la revient effrayer.

39. l. 120:
Lui, né dans les douleurs, roi des infortunés.

41. ll. 1 and 78:
Voilà ce qu'ont chanté les filles d'Israel.

42. ll. 16-22:
Mais le sombre vainqueur marche en baissant la tête;
Sourd à ce bruit de gloire, et seul, silencieux,
Tout à coup il s'arrête, il a fermé ses yeux.
Il a fermé ses yeux, car au loin, de la ville,
Les vierges, en chantant, d'un pas lent et tranquille,
Venaient; il entrevoit le choeur religieux,
C'est pourquoi, plein de crainte, il a fermé ses yeux.

43. ll. 45-46:
. . . le Seigneur n'a-t-il pas
Renversé les cités au seul bruit de vos pas?

44. ll. 51-54:
"Seigneur, vous êtes bien le Dieu de la vengeance;
En échange du crime il vous faut l'innocence.
C'est la vapeur du sang qui plaît au Dieu jaloux!
Je lui dois une hostie, ô ma fille! et c'est vous!"

45. ll. 77-78:
Puis elle vint s'offrir au couteau paternel.
—Voila ce qu'ont chanté les filles d'Israel.

46. ll. 31-32:
"Mon prince, dit quelqu'un, le saint homme est venu.
—Eh! que m'importe, à moi?"

47. ll. 58-60:

LE PRETRE
Le tribunal divin siège dans cette enceinte.
Répondez, le pardon déjà vous est offert;
Dieu même . . .
LE MOURANT
Il est un Dieu? J'ai pourtant bien souffert!

48. ll. 67-84:
LE PRETRE
A la vie, en son nom, dites un mâle adieu.
LE MOURANT
J'étais peut-être Roi.
LE PRETRE
                        Le sauveur était Dieu;
Mais, sans nous élever jusqu'à ce divin Maître,
Si j'osais, après lui, nommer encor le prêtre,
Je vous dirais: Et moi, pour combattre l'enfer,
J'ai resserré mon sein dans un corset de fer;
Mon corps a revêtu l'inflexible cilice,
Où chacun de mes pas trouve un nouveau supplice.
Au cloître est un pavé que, durant quarante ans,
Ont usé chaque jour mes genoux pénitents,
Et c'est encor trop peu que de tant de souffrance
Pour acheter du Ciel l'ineffable espérance.
Au creuset douloureux il faut être épuré
Pour conquérir son rang dans le séjour sacré.
Le temps nous presse, au nom de vos douleurs passées,
Dites-moi vos erreurs pour les voir effacées;
Et devant cette croix où Dieu monta pour nous,
Souhaitez avec moi de tomber à genoux.

49. ll. 95-100:
Un flambeau le révèle entière: ce n'est pas
Un front décoloré par un prochain trépas,
Ce n'est pas l'agonie et son dernier ravage;
Ce qu'il voit est sans traits, et sans vie, et sans âge:
Un fantôme immobile à ses yeux est offert,
Et les feux ont relui sur un masque de fer.

50. ll. 143-48:
Oui, regardez-moi bien, et puis dites après
Qu'un Dieu de l'innocent défend les intérêts;
Des péchés tant proscrits, où toujours l'on succombe,
Aucun n'a séparé mon berceau de ma tombe;
Seul, toujours seul, par l'âge et la douleur vaincu,
Je meurs tout chargé d'ans, et je n'ai pas vécu.

51. ll. 188-208:

"O mon fils! criait-il, votre vie eut son cours;
Heureux, trois fois heureux, celui que Dieu corrige!
Gardons de repousser les peines qu'il inflige:
Voici l'heure où vos maux vous seront précieux,
Il vous a préparé lui-même pour les cieux.
Oubliez votre corps, ne pensez qu'à votre âme;
Dieu lui-même l'a dit: L'homme né de la femme
Ne vit que peu de temps, et c'est dans les douleurs . . .
Me voilà, comme vous, au bout de cette vie . . .
C'est à moi d'envier votre longue souffrance,
Qui d'un monde plus beau vous donne l'espérance;
Les anges à vos pas ouvriront le saint lieu:
Pourvu que vous disiez un mot à votre Dieu,
Il sera satisfait." Ainsi, dans sa parole . . .
Le vieux prêtre engageait le mourant à prier,
Mais en vain.

52. ll. 229-30:

J'ai vu la pitié sur ses lèvres si belles,
Et de ses yeux en pleurs les douces étincelles.

53. ll. 251-60:

LE PRETRE
Non, mon fils, c'est sur vous; voici l'éternité.
LE MOURANT
A moi! je n'en veux pas; j'y trouverais des chaînes.
LE PRETRE
Non, vous n'y trouverez que des faveurs prochaines.
Un mot de repentir, un mot de votre foi,
Le Seigneur vous pardonne.
LE MOURANT

O prêtre! laissez-moi!

LE PRETRE
Dites: Je crois en Dieu. La mort vous est ravie.
LE MOURANT
Laissez en paix ma mort, on y laissa ma vie.
—Et d'un dernier effort l'esclave délirant
Au mur de la prison brise son bras mourant.

54. The English in this quotation is translated from Vigny's
French. The Biblical sources are or seem to be as follows: (a) Ps.
38:1; (b) Ps. 28:3; (c) Ps. 37:32; (d) Job 30:13; (e) Ps. 55:3 (?);
(f) Ps. 130:1; (g) Ps. 59:1 or Ps. 140:1.

55. Canto I, ll. 97-102:

Un jour . . . (Comment oser nommer du nom de jour
Ce qui n'a pas de fuite et n'a pas de retour?

Des langages humains défiant l'indigence,
L'Eternité se voile à notre intelligence,
Et pour nous faire entendre un de ses courts instants,
Il faut chercher pour eux un nom parmi les Temps).
56. *Paradise Lost,* Book V, ll. 579-82:

              . . . when on a day
  (For Time, though in Eternity, appli'd
  To motion, measures all things durable
    By present, past, and future) on such a day . . .
57. Canto I, ll. 106-25:

           . . . le plus beau de nous tous
N'est plus ici; pourtant dans sa vertu première
On le nommait *celui qui porte la lumière;*
Car il portait l'amour et la vie en tout lieu,
Aux astres il portait tous les ordres de Dieu;
La Terre consacrait sa beauté sans égale,
Appelant *Lucifer* l'étoile matinale,
Diamant radieux, que sur son front vermeil,
Parmi ses cheveux d'or a posé le Soleil.
Mais on dit qu'à present il est sans diadème,
Qu'il gémit, qu'il est seul, que personne ne l'aime,
Que la noirceur d'un crime appesantit ses yeux,
Qu'il ne sait plus parler le langage des Cieux;
La mort est dans les mots que prononce sa bouche;
Il brûle ce qu'il voit, il flétrit ce qu'il touche;
Il ne peut plus sentir le mal ni les bienfaits;
Il est même sans joie aux malheurs qu'il a faits.
Le Ciel qu'il habita se trouble à sa mémoire,
Nul Ange n'osera vous conter son histoire,
Aucun Saint n'oserait dire une fois son nom.
58. Canto I, ll. 133-34:
Elle apprit à rêver, et son front innocent
De ce trouble inconnu rougit en s'abaissant.
59. Canto II, l. 12:
La Vierge, en se penchant, croyait voir d'autres Cieux. Cf.
Paradise Lost, Book IV, ll. 456-66, where Eve tells how her first
action had been to fall in love with her own reflected image.
60. Canto II, ll. 85-86:

             . . . l'involontaire flamme
Qui dans un seul regard révèle l'âme à l'âme.
61. Canto II, ll. 136-44:
Je suis celui qu'on aime et qu'on ne connaît pas.
Sur l'homme j'ai fondé mon empire de flamme,
Dans les désirs du coeur, dans les rêves de l'âme,

Dans les liens des corps, attraits mystérieux,
Dans les trésors du sang, dans les regards des yeux.
C'est moi qui fais parler l'épouse dans ses songes;
La jeune fille heureuse apprend d'heureux mensonges;
Je leur donne des nuits qui consolent des jours,
Je suis le Roi secret des secrètes amours.

62. Canto II, ll. 149-54:
J'ai pris au Créateur sa faible créature;;
Nous avons, malgré lui, partagé la Nature:
Je le laisse . . .
Cacher des astres d'or sous l'éclat d'un Soleil;
Moi, j'ai l'ombre muette, et je donne à la terre
La volupté des soirs et les biens du mystère.

63. Canto II, ll. 211-16:
La voilà sous tes yeux l'oeuvre du Malfaiteur;
Ce méchant qu'on accuse est un Consolateur
Qui pleure sur l'esclave et le dérobe au maître,
Le sauve par l'amour des chagrins de son être,
Et dans le mal commun lui-même enseveli,
Lui donne un peu de charme et quelquefois l'oubli.

64. Canto II, ll. 219-20:
Et, luttant par trois fois contre un regard impur,
Une paupière d'or voila ses yeux d'azur.

65. Canto III, ll. 1-16:
D'où venez-vous, Pudeur, noble crainte, ô Mystère,
Qu'au temps de son enfance a vu naître la terre,
Fleur de ses premiers jours qui germez parmi nous,
Rose du Paradis! Pudeur, d'où venez-vous?
Vous pouvez seule encor remplacer l'innocence,
Mais l'arbre défendu vous a donné naissance;
Au charme des vertus votre charme est égal,
Mais vous êtes aussi le premier pas du mal;
D'un chaste vêtement votre sein se décore,
Eve avant le serpent n'en avait pas encore;
Et si le voile pur orne votre maintien,
C'est un voile toujours, et le crime a le sien;
Tout vous trouble, un regard blesse votre paupière,
Mais l'enfant ne craint rien, et cherche la lumière.
Sous ce pouvoir nouveau, la Vierge fléchissait,
Elle tombait déjà, car elle rougissait.

66. Canto III, ll. 40, 50-52:
. . . voilé comme un soleil d'hiver.

. . . la Reine qu'attend mon trône solitaire.
Enfin, par ta présence, habile à me charmer,

Il me fut révélé que je pouvais aimer.
67. Canto III, ll. 81-84:
Mais seul je retournai sous ma belle demeure,
J'y pleurai comme ici, j'y gémis, jusqu'à l'heure
Où le son de ton vol m'émut, me fit trembler,
Comme un prêtre qui sent que son Dieu va parler.
68. Canto III, ll. 109-16:
Puisque vous êtes beau, vous êtes bon, sans doute;
Car, sitôt que des Cieux une âme prend la route,
Comme un saint vêtement, nous voyons sa bonté
Lui donner en entrant l'éternelle beauté.
Mais pourquoi vos discours m'inspirent-ils la crainte?
Pourquoi sur votre front tant de douleur empreinte?
Comment avez-vous pu descendre du saint lieu?
Et comment m'aimez-vous, si vous n'aimez pas Dieu?
69. Canto III, ll. 153-80:
Tel retrouvant ses maux au fond de sa mémoire,
L'Ange maudit pencha sa chevelure noire,
Et se dit, pénétré d'un chagrin infernal:
"—Triste amour du péché! sombres désirs du mal!
De l'orgueil, du savoir gigantesques pensées!
Comment ai-je connu vos ardeurs insensées?
Maudit soit le moment où j'ai mesuré Dieu!
Simplicité du coeur! à qui j'ai dit adieu,
Je tremble devant toi, mais pourtant je t'adore;
Je suis moins criminel puisque je t'aime encore.
Mais dans mon sein flétri tu ne reviendras pas!
Loin de ce que j'étais, quoi! j'ai fait tant de pas!
Et de moi-même à moi si grande est la distance,
Que je ne comprends plus ce que dit l'innocence;
Je souffre, et mon esprit, par le mal abattu,
Ne peut plus remonter jusqu'à tant de vertu.

* * *

Qu'êtes-vous devenus, jours de paix, jours célestes?
Quand j'allais, le premier de ces Anges modestes,
Prier à deux genoux devant l'antique loi,
Et ne pensais jamais au delà de la foi?
L'éternité pour moi s'ouvrait comme une fête;
Et, des fleurs dans mes mains, des rayons sur ma tête,
Je souriais, j'étais . . . J'aurais peut-être aimé!"

* * *

Le Tentateur lui-même était presque charmé,
Il avait oublié son art et sa victime,

Et son coeur un moment se reposa du crime.
Il répétait tout bas, et le front dans ses mains:
"Si je vous connaissais, ô larmes des humains!"

70. *Paradise Lost,* Book IX, l. 465.

71. Canto III, ll. 181-84:
   Ah! si dans ce moment la Vierge eût pu l'entendre.
   Si la céleste main qu'elle eût osé lui tendre
   L'eût saisi repentant, docile à remonter . . .
   Qui sait? le mal peut-être eût cessé d'exister.

72. Canto III, ll. 227-42:
   —Que puis-je faire? hélas! dites, faut-il rester?
   —Oui, descends jusqu'à moi, car je ne puis monter.
   —Mais quel don voulez-vous?—Le plus beau, c'est nous-mêmes.
   Viens.—M'exiler du Ciel?—Qu'importe, si tu m'aimes?
   Touche ma main. Bientôt dans un mépris égal
   Se confondront pour nous et le bien et le mal.
   Tu n'as jamais compris ce qu'on trouve de charmes
   A présenter son sein pour y cacher des larmes.
   Viens, il est un bonheur que moi seul t'apprendrai,
   Tu m'ouvriras ton âme, et je l'y répandrai.
   Comme l'aube et la lune au couchant reposée
   Confondent leurs rayons, ou comme la rosée
   Dans une perle seule unit deux de ses pleurs
   Pour s'empreindre du baume exhalé par les fleurs,
   Comme un double flambeau réunit ses deux flammes,
   Non moins étroitement nous unirons nos âmes.

73. Canto III, ll. 243, 247-49:
   Je t'aime et je descends. Mais que diront les Cieux?

   "Gloire dans l'Univers, dans les Temps, à celui
   Qui s'immole à jamais pour le salut d'autrui."
   Les Cieux semblaient parler. C'en était trop pour elle.

74. Canto III, ll. 262-68:
   J'ai cru t'avoir sauvé.—Non, c'est moi qui t'entraîne.
   —Si nous sommes unis, peu m'importe en quel lieu!
   Nomme-moi donc encor ou ta Soeur ou ton Dieu!
   —J'enlève mon esclave et je tiens ma victime.
   —Tu paraissais si bon! Oh! qu'ai-je fait?—Un crime.
   —Seras-tu plus heureux, du moins, es-tu content?
   —Plus triste que jamais.—Qui donc es-tu? Satan.

75. Canto III, ll. 55-56:
   Soit que ton origine, aussi douce que toi,
   T'ait fait une patrie un peu plus près de moi.

76. Canto I, ll. 177-78:
   Et toujours dans la nuit un rêve lui montrait
   Un Ange malheureux qui de loin l'implorait.

77. Genesis 6:2: "The sons of God saw the daughters of men that they were fair; and they took them wives of all which they chose."

78. Another reference to the story of the destruction of Sodom.

79. Later the same day, it seems. The manipulation of time in this poem is subtle, not to say obscure. Once again, Vigny seems to have forgotten that he is working with the supernatural.

80. ll. 146-50:
   La mort de l'Innocence est pour l'homme un mystère . . .
   La pitié du mortel n'est point celle des Cieux.
   Dieu ne fait point de pacte avec la race humaine;
   Qui créa sans amour fera périr sans haine.

81. l. 332:
   Et l'arc-en-ciel brilla, tout étant accompli.

82. ll. 143-45:
   Va seul au mont Arar, prends ses rocs pour autels,
   Prie, et seul, sans songer au destin des mortels,
   Tiens toujours tes regards plus hauts que sur la Terre.

83. l. 151:
   Sois seul, si Dieu m'entend, je viens.

84. l. 80:
   Ce dernier entretien d'innocence et d'amour.

85. l. 153:
   J'ai monté sur l'Arar, mais avec une femme.

86. ll. 125-34:
   Oh! pourquoi de mes yeux a-t-on levé les voiles?
   Comment ai-je connu le secret des étoiles?
   Science du desert, annales des pasteurs!
   Cette nuit, parcourant vos divines hauteurs
   Dont l'Egypte et Dieu seul [*sic*] connaissent le mystère,
   Je cherchais dans le Ciel l'avenir de la Terre;
   Ma houlette savante, orgueil de nos bergers,
   Traçait l'ordre éternel sur les sables légers,
   Comparant, pour fixer l'heure où l'étoile passe,
   Les cailloux de la plaine aux lueurs de l'espace.

87. l. 39. See also, e. g., ll. 127, 131 just quoted. Cf. Vigny's *Moses*: "As soon as your breath inspired the shepherd [*berger*] . . ."; the Jesus of *Le Mont des oliviers*: "Like a shepherd [*pasteur*] of Egypt he seeks in the firmament . . ."; Samson's tent: "What courageous shepherd [*pasteur*] set it up? . . ."; the poetic-prophetic couple of the *Lettre à Eva* ideally inhabit a "shepherd's house" (*maison du berger*). The figure is common in the contemporary literature. Un-

doubtedly modeled on the Scriptural Good Shepherd, with overtones of the Homeric Shepherd of the Peoples, it is a good, if hackneyed, image for the poet-*vates* conception which obsesses Vigny.

88. l. 162:

> Ah! louons l'Eternel, il punit, mais rassemble!

89. ll. 1-5, 16-20:

> La Terre était riante et dans sa fleur première;
> Le jour avait encor cette même lumière
> Qui du Ciel embelli couronna les hauteurs
> Quand Dieu la fit tomber de ses doigts créateurs.
> Rien n'avait dans sa forme altéré la nature . . .
> Chaque trésor restait dans l'élément natal,
> Sans enfreindre jamais la céleste défense;
> Et la beauté du monde attestait son enfance;
> Tout suivait sa loi douce et son premier penchant,
> Tout était pur encor.

90. l. 20:

> Mais l'homme était méchant.

91. ll. 81-88:

> Comme la Terre est belle en sa rondeur immense!
> La vois-tu qui s'étend jusqu'où le Ciel commence?
> La vois-tu s'embellir de toutes ses couleurs? . . .
> On dirait aujourd'hui que les vastes campagnes
> Elèvent leur encens, étalent leur beauté,
> Pour toucher, s'il se peut, le Seigneur irrité.

92. ll. 89-97:

> Mais les vapeurs du Ciel, comme de noirs fantômes,
> Amènent tous ces bruits, ces lugubres symptômes
> Qui devaient, sans manquer au moment attendu,
> Annoncer l'agonie à l'Univers perdu.
> Viens, tandis que l'horreur partout nous environne,
> Et qu'une vaste nuit lentement nous couronne,
> Viens, ô ma bien-aimée! et, fermant tes beaux yeux,
> Qu'épouvante l'aspect du désordre des Cieux,
> Sur mon sein, sous mes bras repose encor ta tête.

93. ll. 99-100:

> Je te dirai l'instant où le Ciel sourira,
> Et durant le péril ma voix te parlera.

94. This despite religious tradition and Holy Writ, both of which Vigny alters in this poem and elsewhere. The rainbow does not await the recession of the waters, but shines at the moment when the earth is completely engulfed. Cf. the hero's great strength, in *La Colère de Samson,* which enables him to pull down the temple

on the very day of his capture, and which thus can in no way depend upon the growth of his hair.

95. This achievement may be equalled by such passages as the monologue of Auguste in Corneille's *Cinna*, or the apostrophe of Racine's *Phèdre* to Minos, or again in the opening scene of his *Athalie*. Vigny himself comes close in the third part of *La Maison du Berger*. Other readers will cite other poems, but not many. *Moïse* is a rare accomplishment in French prosody.

96. Letter to Camilla Maunoir, December 27, 1838, published by P. Godet in *Revue de Paris*, 1897, p. 677. I have been scolded for implying that this passage, written presumably some sixteen years after the poem, may be taken as stating Vigny's original intention. It seems to me, regardless of date, that the statement squares perfectly with the manifest intention of the *Poèmes antiques et modernes*.

97. l. 51:
Que vous ai-je donc fait pour être votre élu?

98. ll. 91-92:
Sitôt que votre souffle a rempli le berger,
Les hommes se sont dit: Il nous est étranger.
l. 95:
J'ai vu l'amour s'éteindre et l'amitié tarir.
ll. 100-101:
Pour dormir sur un sein mon front est trop pesant,
Ma main laisse l'effroi sur la main qu'elle touche.
ll. 103-4:
Aussi, loin de m'aimer, voilà qu'ils tremblent tous,
Et, quand j'ouvre les bras, on tombe à mes genoux.

99. ll. 113-14:
Bientôt le haut du mont reparut sans Moïse.—
Il fut pleuré.

100. ll. 109-12:
Des vers de fou, sans rime et sans mesure.—Un mot
Qui n'avait pas de suite était tout seul en haut;
Demande sans réponse, énigme inextricable,
Question sur la mort.

101. E. g., Hugo's celebrated panorama in *Notre-Dame de Paris*; Balzac's presentation of Rastignac in the cemetery of Père Lachaise at the end of *Le Père Goriot* (1831 and 1834 respectively).

102. l. 13.

103. ll. 41-42:
—Oui, c'est bien une Roue;; et c'est la main de Dieu
Qui tient et fait mouvoir son invisible essieu.

104. ll. 45-54:
Quand la vivante Roue hésite dans ses tours,

Tout hésite et s'étonne, et recule en son cours,
Les rayons effrayés disent au cercle: Arrête.
Il le dit à son tour aux cercles dont le crête
S'enchâsse dans la sienne et tourne sous sa loi.
L'un le redit à l'autre; et l'impassible roi,
Paris, l'axe immortel, Paris, l'axe du monde,
Puise ses mouvements dans sa vigueur profonde,
Les communique à tous, les imprime à chacun,
Les impose de force, et n'en reçoit aucun.

105. ll. 67-68:
Car Paris l'éternel de leurs efforts se joue,
Et le moyeu divin tournerait sans la Roue.

106. ll. 73-74:
—C'est donc bien, Voyageur, une Roue en effet.
Le vertige parfois est prophétique.

107. ll. 235-58:
—Je ne sais d'assurés, dans le chaos du sort,
Que deux points seulement, LA SOUFFRANCE ET LA MORT
Tous les hommes y vont avec toutes les villes.
Mais les cendres, je crois, ne sont jamais stériles.
Si celles de Paris un jour sur ton chemin
Se trouvent, pèse-les, et prends-nous dans ta main,
Et, voyant à la place une rase campagne,
Dis: Le volcan a fait éclater sa montagne!
Pense au triple labeur que je t'ai révélé,
Et songe qu'au dessus de ceux dont j'ai parlé
Il en fut de meilleurs et de plus purs encore,
Rares parmi tous ceux dont leur temps se décore,
Que la foule admirait et blâmait à moitié,
Des hommes pleins d'amour, de doute et de pitié,
Qui disaient: *Je ne sais,* des choses de la vie,
Dont le pouvoir ou l'or ne fut jamais l'envie,
Et qui, par dévouement, sans détourner les yeux,
Burent jusqu'a la lie un calice odieux.
[The wishful self-portrait in the foregoing eight lines is inescapable.]
—Ensuite, Voyageur, tu quitteras l'enceinte,
Tu jetteras au vent cette poussiére éteinte,
Puis, levant seul ta voix dans le désert sans bruit,
Tu crîras: *"Pour longtemps le monde est dans la nuit!"*

Chapter Three

1. *Chatterton,* in prose, is a peculiar case which will presently be
examined. *Stello* and particularly *Daphné* are extremely interesting

to Vigny specialists. Both are better written than *Cinq-Mars* or *L'Alméh*, but neither, it seems to me, so clearly shows us the artist at work. For this reason they are not considered here.

2. Presumably a reference to the narcissus considered as a narcotic. See, e. g., Robert Graves, *The Greek Myths*, 85:1.

3. ll. 39-48, 53-56:

L'Homme a toujours besoin de caresse et d'amour;
Sa mère l'en abreuve alors qu'il vient au jour,
Et ce bras le premier l'engourdit, le balance
Et lui donne un désir d'amour et d'indolence.
Troublé dans l'action, troublé dans le dessein,
Il rêvera partout à la chaleur du sein,
Aux chansons de la nuit, aux baisers de l'aurore,
A la lèvre de feu que sa lèvre dévore,
Aux cheveux dénoués qui roulent sur son front,
Et les regrets du lit, en marchant, le suivront. . . .
Quand le combat que Dieu fit pour la créature
Et contre son semblable et contre la Nature
Force l'Homme à chercher un sein où reposer,
Quand ses yeux sont en pleurs, il lui faut un baiser.

All references to *Les Destinées* are to the critical edition by V. L. Saulnier (*Textes Littéraires Français*). (Paris, 1947)

4. ll. 7-9, 13-15:

Ces froides déités liaient le joug de plomb
Sur le crâne et les yeux des Hommes leurs esclaves,
Tous errants, sans étoile, en un désert sans fond . . .

Tristes divinités du monde oriental,
Femmes au voile blanc, immuables statues,
Elles nous écrasaient de leur poids colossal.

5. ll. 22-24:

Un soir, il arriva que l'antique planète
Secoua sa poussière.—Il se fit un grand cri:
"Le Sauveur est venu." . . .

ll. 25-27:

Il a le front sanglant et le côté meurtri,
Mais la Fatalité meurt au pied du Prophète:
La Croix monte et s'étend sur nous comme un abri!

ll. 31-33:

Détachant les noeuds lourds du joug de plomb du Sort,
Toutes les Nations à la fois s'écrièrent:
"O Seigneur! est-il vrai? le Destin est-il mort?"

6. ll. 82-85, 88-90:

Retournez en mon nom, Reines, je suis la Grâce.

L'Homme sera toujours un nageur incertain
Dans les ondes du temps qui se mesure et passe.

Vous toucherez son front, ô filles du Destin! . . .

Il sera plus heureux, se croyant maître et libre,
En luttant contre vous dans un combat mauvais
Où moi seule d'en haut je tiendrai l'équilibre.

7. ll. 101-5:
—Mais, plus forte à présent, dans ce sombre duel,
Notre âme en deuil combat ces Esprits impassibles.

Nous soulevons parfois leur doigt faux et cruel.
La Volonté transporte à des hauteurs sublimes
Notre front éclairé par un rayon du ciel.

8. ll. 119-23:
Question sans réponse où vos Saints se sont tus!
O Mystère! ô tourment de l'âme forte et grave!

Notre mot éternel est-il: C'ETAIT ECRIT?
SUR LE LIVRE DE DIEU, dit l'Orient esclave;
Et l'Occident répond: SUR LE LIVRE DU CHRIST.

9. Vigny is thinking notably of the reactionary Joseph de Maistre.

10. ll. 87-90:
Mal et Doute! En un mot je puis les mettre en poudre.
. . . laissez-moi vous absoudre
De les avoir permis.—C'est l'accusation
Qui pèse de partout sur la création!

11. ll. 133-34:
Mais il renonce et dit: "Que votre volonté
Soit faite et non la mienne et pour l'éternité!"

12. ll. 143-49:
S'il est vrai qu'au Jardin sacré des Ecritures,
Le fils de l'Homme ait dit ce qu'on voit rapporté;
Muet, aveugle et sourd au cri des créatures,
Si le Ciel nous laissa comme un monde avorté,
Le juste opposera le dédain à l'absence,
Et ne répondra plus que par un froid silence
Au silence éternel de la Divinité.

13. l. 225.

14. The form is rare in French verse, both before and after Vigny. He uses it for five of the eleven poems in *Les Destinées*: *La Maison du Berger*, *Les Oracles*, *La Bouteille à la mer*, *Wanda*, *L'Esprit pur*.

15. ll. 227-38:
Sais-tu que, pour punir l'homme, sa créature,
D'avoir porté la main sur l'arbre du savoir,

Dieu permit qu'avant tout, de l'amour de soi-même
En tout temps, à tout âge, il fît son bien suprême,
Tourmenté de s'aimer, tourmenté de se voir?

Mais si Dieu près de lui t'a voulu mettre, ô femme!
Compagne délicate! Eva! sais-tu pourquoi?
C'est pour qu'il se regarde au miroir d'une autre âme,
Qu'il entende ce chant qui ne vient que de toi:
—L'enthousiasme pur dans une voix suave.
C'est afin que tu sois son juge et son esclave
Et règnes sur sa vie en vivant sous sa loi.

16. l. 246:
Ta pensée a des bonds comme ceux des gazelles.

17. ll. 253-54, 257-61:
Mais aussi tu n'as rien de nos lâches prudences,
Ton coeur vibre et résonne au cri de l'opprimé. . . .
Tes paroles de feu meuvent les multitudes,
Tes pleurs lavent l'injure et les ingratitudes,
Tu pousses par le bras l'homme . . . il se lève armé.

C'est à toi qu'il convient d'ouïr les grandes plaintes
Que l'humanité triste exhale sourdement.

18. ll. 246-52:
Ta pensée a des bonds comme ceux des gazelles,
Mais ne saurait marcher sans guide et sans appui.
Le sol meurtrit ses pieds, l'air fatigue ses ailes,
Son oeil se ferme au jour dès que le jour a lui;
Parfois, sur les hauts lieux d'un seul élan posée,
Troublée au bruit des vents, ta mobile pensée
Ne peut seule y veiller sans crainte et sans ennui.

19. ll. 274-80:
Eva, j'aimerai tout dans les choses créées,
Je les contemplerai dans ton regard rêveur
Qui partout répandra ses flammes colorées,
Son repos gracieux, sa magique saveur:
Sur mon coeur déchiré viens poser ta main pure,
Ne me laisse jamais seul avec la Nature:
Car je la connais trop pour n'en pas avoir peur.

20. Cf., e. g., the Parnassian Hérédia, whose Antony witnesses his own defeat at Actium reflected in the eyes of Cleopatra.

21. ll. 281-301.
ll. 288-89:
Je roule avec dédain, sans voir et sans entendre,
A côté des fourmis vos populations.

l. 292:
On me dit une mère, et je suis une tombe.

22. ll. 302-8. Line 308 reads:
Aimez ce que jamais on ne verra deux fois.

23. ll. 330-36:
Nous marcherons ainsi, ne laissant que notre ombre
Sur cette terre ingrate où les morts ont passé;
Nous nous parlerons d'eux à l'heure où tout est sombre,
Où tu te plais à suivre un chemin effacé,
A rêver, appuyée aux branches incertaines,
Pleurant, comme Diane au bord de ses fontaines,
Ton amour taciturne et toujours menacé.

24. ll. 316-22:
Vivez, froide Nature, et revivez sans cesse
Sous nos pieds, sur nos fronts, puisque c'est votre loi;·
Vivez, et dédaignez, si vous êtes déesse,
L'Homme, humble passager, qui dut vous être un roi;
Plus que tout votre règne et que ses splendeurs vaines,
J'aime la majesté des souffrances humaines,
Vous ne recevrez pas un cri d' amour de moi.

25. Cf. the following passage from the *Pensées* of Pascal (a part of No. 434 in the Brunschvicq ordering): " What a chimaera then is man? What a novelty, what a monster, what a chaos, what a subject of contradiction, what a prodigy! Judge of all things, imbecile earthworm; repository of the true, sewer of uncertainty and error; glory and filth of the universe."

"Quelle chimère est-ce donc que l'homme? Quelle nouveauté, quel monstre, quel chaos, quel sujet de contradiction, quel prodige! Juge de toutes choses, imbécile ver de terre; dépositaire du vrai, cloaque d'incertitude et d'erreur; gloire et rebut de l'univers."

26. ll. 1-7:
Si ton coeur, gémissant du poids de notre vie,
Se traîne et se débat comme un aigle blessé,
Portant comme le mien, sur son aile asservie,
Tout un monde fatal, écrasant et glacé;
S'il ne bat qu'en saignant par sa plaie immortelle,
S'il ne voit plus l'amour, son étoile fidèle,
Eclairer pour lui seul l'horizon effacé . . .

27. ll. 22-28:
Pars courageusement, laisse toutes les villes;
Ne ternis plus tes pieds aux poudres du chemin,
Du haut de nos pensers vois les cités serviles

Comme les rocs fatals de l'esclavage humain.
Les grands bois et les champs sont de vastes asiles,
Libres comme la mer autour des sombres îles.
Marche à travers les champs une fleur à la main.

28. ll. 43-46:
Il est sur la montagne une épaisse bruyère
Où les pas du chasseur ont peine à se plonger,
Qui plus haut que nos fronts lève sa tête altière,
Et garde dans la nuit le pâtre et l'étranger.

29. l. 47:
Viens y cacher l'amour et ta divine faute.

30. ll. 48-49:
Si l'herbe est agitée ou n'est pas assez haute,
J'y roulerai pour toi la Maison du Berger.

31. The image may have been unwittingly suggested by Marie Dorval, who, touring the provinces, had complained in a letter to Vigny of the discomforts of riding sitting up in a coach in bad repair, and wished that she might travel in a *maison de berger*.

32. ll. 50-56:
Elle va doucement avec ses quatre roues,
Son toit n'est pas plus haut que ton front et tes yeux;
La couleur du corail et celle de tes joues
Teignent le char nocturne et ses muets essieux.
Le seuil est parfumé, l'alcôve est large et sombre,
Et, là, parmi les fleurs, nous trouverons dans l'ombre,
Pour nos cheveux unis, un lit silencieux.

33. ll. 57-63:
Je verrai, si tu veux, les pays de la neige,
Ceux où l'astre amoureux dévore et resplendit,
Ceux que heurtent les vents, ceux que la mer assiège,
Ceux où le pôle obscur sous sa glace est maudit.
Nous suivrons du hasard la course vagabonde.
Que m'importe le jour, que m'importe le monde?
Je dirai qu'ils sont beaux quand tes yeux l'auront dit.

34. ll. 64-124, *passim*.

35. ll. 127-33:
Jamais la Rêverie amoureuse et paisible
N'y verra sans horreur son pied blanc attaché;
Car il faut que ses yeux sur chaque objet visible
Versent un long regard, comme un fleuve épanché;
Qu'elle interroge tout avec inquiétude,
Et, des secrets divins se faisant une étude,
Marche, s'arrête et marche avec le col penché.

36. ll. 197-208:

Comment se garderaient les profondes pensées
Sans rassembler leurs feux dans ton diamant pur
Qui conserve si bien leurs splendeurs condensées?
Ce fin miroir solide, étincelant et dur,
Reste des nations mortes, durable pierre
Qu'on trouve sous ses pieds lorsque dans la poussière
On cherche les cités sans en voir un seul mur.

Diamant sans rival, que tes feux illuminent
Les pas lents et tardifs de l'humaine Raison!
Il faut, pour voir de loin les peuples qui cheminent,
Que le Berger t'enchâsse au toit de sa Maison.

37. ll. 208-24:

Le jour n'est pas levé.—Nous en sommes encore
Au premier rayon blanc qui précède l'aurore
Et dessine la terre aux bords de l'horizon.

Les peuples tout enfants à peine se découvrent
Par-dessus les buissons nés pendant leur sommeil,
Et leur main, à travers les ronces qu'ils entr'ouvrent,
Met aux coups mutuels le premier appareil.
La barbarie encor tient nos pieds dans sa gaîne.
Le marbre des vieux temps jusqu'aux reins nous enchaîne,
Et tout homme énergique au dieu Terme est pareil.

Mais notre esprit rapide en mouvements abonde;
Ouvrons tout l'arsenal de ses puissants ressorts.
L'invisible est réel. Les âmes ont leur monde
Où sont accumulés d'impalpables trésors.
Le Seigneur contient tout dans ses deux bras immenses,
Son Verbe est le séjour de nos intelligences,
Comme ici-bas l'espace est celui de nos corps.

38. His reasons, at least those that he declares, are less poetic than they are Victorian.

39. ll. 120-32:

Votre souffle était juste et votre chant est faux.
Pour moi qui ne sais rien et vais du doute au rêve,
Je crois qu'après la mort, quand l'union s'achève,
L'âme retrouve alors la vue et la clarté,
Et que, jugeant son oeuvre avec sérénité,
Comprenant sans obstacle et s'expliquant sans peine,
Comme ses soeurs du ciel elle est puissante et reine,
Se mesure au vrai poids, connaît visiblement

Que son souffle était faux par le faux instrument,
N'était ni glorieux, ni vil, n'étant pas libre;
Que le corps seulement empêchait l'équilibre;
Et, calme, elle reprend, dans l'idéal bonheur,
La sainte égalité des esprits du Seigneur.

40. l. 140:
La note était plus juste et le souffle assuré.

41. See Saulnier's introduction to the poem (pp. 131-43).

42. Vigny's date is 1853.

43. ll. 4-7:
Oubliez les enfants par la mort arrêtés;
Oubliez Chatterton, Gilbert et Malfilâtre;
De l'oeuvre d'avenir saintement idolâtre,
Enfin, oubliez l'homme en vous-même.—Ecoutez.

44. ll. 168-70, 176:
Sur la pierre des morts croît l'arbre de grandeur.
Cet arbre est le plus beau de la terre promise,
C'est votre phare à tous, Penseurs laborieux! . . .

Le vrai Dieu, le Dieu fort, est le Dieu des idées.

45. ll. 1-7:
Si l'orgueil prend ton coeur quand le peuple me nomme,
Que de mes livres seuls te vienne ta fierté,
J'ai mis sur le cimier doré du gentilhomme
Une plume de fer qui n'est pas sans beauté.
J'ai fait illustre un nom qu'on m'a transmis sans gloire.
Qu'il soit ancien, qu'importe? il n'aura de mémoire
Que du jour seulement où mon front l'a porté.

46. ll. 43-49:
Tous sont morts en laissant leur nom sans auréole:
Mais sur le disque d'or voilà qu'il est écrit,
Disant: "Ici passaient deux races de la Gaule
Dont le dernier vivant monte au temple et s'inscrit,
Non sur l'obscur amas des vieux noms inutiles
Des orgueilleux méchants et des riches futiles,
Mais sur le pur tableau des titres de L'ESPRIT."

47. ll. 54-56:
L'ECRIT UNIVERSEL, parfois impérissable,
Que tu graves au marbre ou traînes sur le sable,
Colombe au bec d'airain! VISIBLE SAINT-ESPRIT!

48. ll. 57-63:
Seul et dernier anneau de deux chaînes brisées,
Je reste. Et je soutiens encor dans les hauteurs,

> Parmi les maîtres purs de nos savants musées,
> L'IDEAL du poète et des graves penseurs.
> J'éprouve sa durée en vingt ans de silence,
> Et toujours, d'âge en âge encor, je vois la France
> Contempler mes tableaux et leur jeter des fleurs.

49. Vigny does not capitalize; clearly he is punning upon his book title and the fate of his work in general.

50. ll. 64-70:

> Jeune postérité d'un vivant qui vous aime!
> Mes traits dans vos regards ne sont pas effacés;
> Je peux en ce miroir *me connaître moi-même,*
> Juge toujours nouveau de nos travaux passés!
> Flots d'amis renaissants! Puissent mes destinées
> Vous amener à moi, de dix en dix années,
> Attentifs à mon oeuvre, et pour moi c'est assez!

51. With an introduction in *Les Belles Lectures,* January 24, 1946.

52. "Apparently"—not all of Vigny's known manuscripts have yet been published; and it is always possible that unknown ones may exist.

53. II, 672.

54. II, 566.

55. Let the irreverent reader remember that *The Pirates of Penzance* did not appear until 1879.

56. II, 619.

57. II, 650.

58. II, 661.

59. II, 662.

60. Vigny himself did this. Renaud is another of his self-idealizations.

61. Chapter V (II, 625-37).

62. II, 674.

63. II, 675.

64. *Ibid.* Emphasis added.

65. II, 676.

Chapter Four

1. "Reflets de nacre": *nacre* is mother-of-pearl. It is extremely difficult to translate Gautier's French here; he writes the language of poetry.

2. September 28, 1863; quoted by Ernest Dupuy, *Alfred de Vigny, ses amitiés, son rôle littéraire* (Paris, 1910), I, 392-93.

3. The spectacular example is his candidacy for the French Academy and the circumstances of his taking his seat there in 1846.

Bibliography

The following list is a summary one made for the general reader. Its intentions are to refer him to some useful editions of Vigny's works, to the fullest available bibliographies of writings by and about Vigny, and to a few important studies (not one of them, unfortunately, in English).

I. Bibliographies
The most nearly complete bibliography of writings by and about Vigny may be compiled from the following:
Thieme, *Bibliographie de la littérature française de 1800 à 1930.* Paris: Droz, 1933; and from its continuations; under the same title and by the same publisher:
Dreher and Rolli, 1930-39.
Drevet and Thieme, 1940-49.
Publications from 1950 to the present can be located in the quarterly bibliographies of *La Revue d'histoire littéraire de la France* (*RHLF*) and *La Revue de littérature comparée* (*RLC*); also in the annual bibliographies of *PMLA*.

II. Primary Sources
A. TRANSLATIONS
Chatterton. Tr. W. Hazlitt. London: D. Bogue, 1847.
Cinq-Mars. Tr. W. Hazlitt. London: D. Bogue, 1847. Republished Boston: Little, Brown, 1889.
The Spider and the Fly (Cinq-Mars). Tr. M. Pemberton. Philadelphia: David McKay, n. d. [1925].
Military Servitude and Grandeur. Tr. F. W. Huard. New York: Doran, n. d. (1919).
I know of no English translations of any of Vigny's verse.
B. EDITIONS
A really complete edition of Vigny's works does not exist; I list the two best approximations thereto:
Alfred de Vigny, *Oeuvres complètes.* Ed. F. Baldensperger. Paris: Conard, 1914-35, 7 vols.
——, *Oeuvres complètes.* Ed. F. Baldensperger. Paris: NRF, 1948 (second printing, 1955) [*Bibliothèque de la Pléiade*], 2 vols. See my Chapter 2, note 1.

C. "INDIVIDUAL" EDITIONS

Alfred de Vigny, *Poèmes antiques et modernes.* Ed. E. Estève. Paris: Droz, 1931.

——, *Les Destinées.* Ed. V. L. Saulnier. Paris: Droz, 1947.

——, *Chatterton.* Ed. L. Petroni. Bologna: Prof. Riccardo, 1962.

(Note: The foregoing are critical editions in the grand French manner.)

——, *Mémoires inédits, fragments et projets.* Ed. J. Sangnier. Paris: Gallimard, 1958. See my Chapter 2, note 2.

III. Secondary Sources

Bonnefoy, G. *La Pensée religieuse et morale d'Alfred de Vigny.* Paris: Hachette, 1944. See my Chapter 2, note 19. The content and the worth of this book far transcend its title.

Castex, P. G. *Vigny, l'homme et l'oeuvre.* Paris: Boivin, 1952. The handiest concise treatment of its title, comporting also chronologies and a summary bibliography.

Citoleux, M. *Alfred de Vigny, persistances et affinités étrangères.* Paris: Champion, 1924. A thorough French doctoral thesis of its time, ponderously replete with vast information, and therefore extremely useful.

Dorval, Marie. *Lettres à Alfred de Vigny.* Ed. C. Gaudier. Paris: Gallimard, 1942. Just what it says it is, without apparatus. Fascinating when set beside the journal and the correspondence of Vigny.

Dupuy, E. *La Jeunesse des Romantiques.* Paris: Oudin, 1905. Old-fashioned, charmingly written, anecdotal, above all very well-documented.

——, *Alfred de Vigny, ses amitiés, son rôle littéraire.* Paris: 1910–12, 2 vols. Detailed expansion of the Vigny portion of the previous item. Excellent documentation. Critical portion dated, as whose is not?

Flottes, P. *La Pensée politique et sociale d'Alfred de Vigny.* Paris, 1927. A companion piece to the Bonnefoy (*supra*). Scrupulous and excellent realization of its title.

Germain, F. *L'Imagination d'Alfred de Vigny.* Paris: Corti, 1961. An incredibly thorough and detailed examination of Vigny's uses of language, image, and style, accompanied by a very full bibliography pertinent to the subject in general and Vigny in particular. To date the most fully detailed study of Vigny as a writer.

Guillemin, H. *M. de Vigny, homme d'ordre et poète.* Paris: Gallimard, 1955. A set of unpublished writings by Vigny, preceded by an impish (and therefore refreshing—most Vigny studies seem to lack this quality) presentation, with documents, of the servant of mankind as a toady to Napoleon III.

Lauvrière, E. *Alfred de Vigny, sa vie et son oeuvre*. Paris: Grasset, 1945. To date the most detailed, the most fully documented biography of Vigny. I do not think it is a very good book, but its documentation is unequalled in the Vigny bibliography.

Whitridge, A. *Alfred de Vigny*. London and New York: Oxford, 1933. The only book-length presentation in English of Vigny that I have found. It is very short, very superficial, and full of factual errors.

Index